Fracking the Neighborhood

Urban and Industrial Environments

series editor: Robert Gottlieb, Henry R. Luce Professor of Urban and Environmental Policy, Occidental College

For a complete list of the series, see the back of the book.

Fracking the Neighborhood

Reluctant Activists and Natural Gas Drilling

Jessica Smartt Gullion

The MIT Press
Cambridge, Massachusetts
London, England

Set in Stone Sans and Stone Serif by Toppan Best-set Premedia Limited. Printed on recycled paper and bound in the United States of America.

Library of Congress Cataloging-in-Publication Data

Gullion, Jessica Smartt, 1972- Fracking the neighborhood : reluctant activists and natural gas drilling / Jessica Smartt Gullion.
   pages cm.—(Urban and industrial environments)
Includes bibliographical references and index.
ISBN 978-0-262-02976-6 (hardcover : alk. paper)
1. Gas wells—Hydraulic fracturing—Environmental aspects—United States.
2. Urban pollution—United States. 3. Environmentalism. 4. Urban ecology (Sociology)   I. Title
TD195.G3G864   2015
622'.3381—dc23

                                                              2015011499

10   9   8   7   6   5   4   3   2   1

I think this is going to be one of the biggest environmental disasters in our history.
—natural gas drilling activist

Personally, I think that all environmental issues are human issues really.
—natural gas drilling activist

Contents

Preface (a prose poem*)

The ground trembles beneath my bare feet. Truck after truck rumbles up my
    street, hauling crack/frack fluid (water, chemicals) to the natural gas
    drilling site at the end of my block.
Injecting their fluid into the earth.
Penetrating, cracking her open.
She rumbles.
We've had three earthquakes in so many days. A man in a gray suit comes
    on TV. He says the earthquakes aren't related to the drilling. (Never mind
    we never had quakes here before).
I live in the middle of the Barnett Shale, in a suburban town not far from
    Dallas. Tucked in my neighborhood are natural gas pads. Pipelines criss-
    cross behind our fences. There are more than three hundred sites in
    town.
Air alert! It's a Red Day. The children cannot play outside; the air is danger-
    ous to breathe. They ask to go swimming—Mama, it's summer, it's hot
    out. No, I tell them, let's go after dinner when there is shade. I don't tell
    them breathing outside is deadly (I don't want to frighten them).
The drill towers about a hundred feet above our homes. They call it a Christ-
    mas Tree, but there's nothing festive about it.
Jenny, the woman across the street, found a lump in her breast. She has
    Stage Three Breast Cancer. Jenny is 29.
Elizabeth lives two houses down. Her daughter has leukemia and has no
    hair. The PTA had a fund raiser to help them pay for chemo. Then Char-
    lie's daughter was diagnosed. And then Tori's son.

*by Jessica Smartt Gullion; first published as "Toxic Neighborhood," *Qualitative
Inquiry* 19, no. 7 (2013): 491–492

Our spare change won't go that far.

So many of our neighbors have cancer that the school district started a support group. It meets at our elementary school.

The Texas Department of State Health Services says we are a statistical anomaly, not a cancer cluster.

Nothing to see here, folks. Move along.

Some of our neighbors tried to organize against the gas companies. We don't care that they drill here, we said, but we want them to be safe about it. There is An Activist who comes to our meetings with a dummy dressed in overalls and a gas mask. She calls him Ben Zene, because benzene is always at the gas sites and she doesn't want anyone to forget. You learn all about these chemicals and how they cause cancer when these things come into your neighborhood. It's like being Erin Brockovich.

We protested at the site. We wore paper gas masks and put paper gas masks on our children. We had signs—Get the Frack Out of Our Town! and Fracking Pollutes! and Our Children Can't Breathe! We tied the signs to the fence. The next day we found our signs vandalized with drawings of genitalia.

Pussy, one said.

You're next.

We watch the commercials, a man in pressed jeans, cowboy boots. He's someone famous. He stands in a lush pasture, show horses graze in the background. He tells us natural gas will bring jobs and that it is a greener alternative. The camera zooms in on the top of a drill. Someone has attached an American Flag, it flutters in the breeze. Natural gas will free us from dependence on foreign oil, the nice-looking man says. We will finally be free.

My cousin berates me for being unpatriotic when I complain. Give me a break, he says, where do you think electricity comes from? He throws up his hands in disgust.

I feel small.

I just want them to do it safely, I whisper.

I don't want my kids to get cancer.

There's this blogger I read. She lives just a few miles from my house, in a neighboring town. She started seeing weird stuff in her yard, what looked like bubbling frack fluid, in her yard. She's on well water and she had her water tested. It was contaminated with all sorts of chemicals.

She tried to light her water on fire, like they do in that documentary, *Gasland*. She video-taped it and put it on her blog. She filled the basin and tried to light it. The water didn't catch fire, but after she'd held the flame to the water, she swished her hand around in it. When she pulled° her hand out, there was a film hanging from it, it looked just like Saran Wrap.

That's petrochemicals. If you can make plastic with flame, you have petrochemicals in your water.

The blogger tried to sell her house, but after the wells went in her property value dropped by seventy-five percent. No one will buy these houses. We are trapped.

I call the city: We can't help you.

I call the health department: We can't help you.

I call the Texas Commission on Environmental Quality: We can't help you.

I call the Railroad Commission: We can't help you.

I call the Environmental Protection Agency: We can't help you.

I call my Senator: We can't help you.

I am surrounded by a lack of competent guardians.

I put down the phone.

Grass fires burn along the freeway. Fields of corn crumble to dust. My flowerbed withers and browns. We are under Stage Four Drought Rationing. We cannot water the lawns.

Meanwhile five million gallons of water are diverted to crack/frack the well up the block. Five million gallons lost, contaminated with chemicals and radiation. Any water that flows back up to the surface will be hauled back out by those trucks to an empty well and injected thousands of feet below ground, lost to our generation and generations to come.

The ground trembles beneath my bare feet. Truck after truck rumbles up my street, hauling crack/frack fluid (water, chemicals) to the natural gas drilling site at the end of my block.

I wipe my nose with the back of my hand. It is bleeding again.

Acknowledgments

A project of this scope does not happen in isolation, and I am appreciative of all those who helped and supported me through this journey.

The research on which the book is based would not have happened without the support of environmental activists in the Barnett Shale. Thank you to all of the activists and other participants in this story. Your willingness to stand up for the community and your continued fight for health and well-being is an inspiration.

I would like to thank Kathy Jack for her assistance and insights, and for her constant encouragement. Thanks also to Rosemary Candelario for help with the book proposal, and to Tom Guffey and Dian Werhane-Jordan for assistance with transcription. Much appreciation also for Dona Perkins and Jessica Williams' help in the final stages. Gabrielle Calvocoressi's listserv support group The Year I Wrote the Book was a lifesaver, and helped me to crank out more words when I thought I had none left.

Thank you to both Claire Sahlin and Jim Williams for instrumental conversations along the way, and to the rest of my colleagues in the Sociology and Social Work Department and the Women's Studies Department at Texas Woman's University for your support. Thank you to my friend Beth Fawcett; discussing method and research ethics was always better over the "wet rock tea." Jimmie Lynn Harris, a fantastic reference librarian at the TWU library, your skills added gems of detail I never would have found on my own. I would also like to express my appreciation to the participants in the International Congress on Qualitative Inquiry who offered encouragement for my work. Thank you also to all my friends and colleagues who checked in on how things were going and who gave me a "You can do it babe!" when I felt I could not write any more.

Many thanks to Miranda Martin and Paul Bethge at the MIT Press for supporting and encouraging this project and for pushing me to develop the manuscript, and to the anonymous reviewers for feedback. It's a better book because of you.

This book is dedicated to my mom, Kathleen Smartt. A consummate activist, she taught me from a young age to demand justice and that sometimes you need to fight City Hall. She taught me the importance of speaking up against all forms of oppression, and that it is the responsibility of all members of society to participate in the world around them rather than being passive witnesses to atrocities.

Most of all, thank you to Greg, Renn, and Rory. Nothing happens without you. You are my love and light.

Introduction

I drive down the narrow tree-lined road to Joyce's house. Rounding a bend, I encounter an industrial scene. Behind a chain-link fence, a natural gas drilling rig extends about 200 feet up into the aquamarine sky. There are tanks, compressors, pipes, and diesel trucks spilling black smoke, all fenced in with barbed wire. Joyce has left the gate open for me.

The modest house is set back from the road. A pack of dogs run up to my car. They wag their tails and bark. Maneuvering slowly up the drive, I'm afraid of running over one of them, but they scamper out of my way.

I park and step onto the gravel, and the dogs bark and run up to meet me. A woman's voice calls to them, and I see Joyce step off the porch and walk toward me.

"No one will sneak up on us, out here with these dogs," she says with a laugh before inviting me inside.

We sit at Joyce's kitchen table. Through a large bay window I can see a tree-surrounded pond at the bottom of a hill. A pipe siphons water from the pond and carries it up a slight hill on the opposite side of the pond to the pad site (that is, the entire site of the operation) of a natural gas well. I can hear the rumble of a compressor through the glass. A soft rattle comes from the pane as the compressor sucks gas through the steel pipes. The window over the sink is filled with the sight of the drilling rig I drove by on my way in.

Joyce's home sits in the middle of three natural gas sites. One of the pads is 200 feet from her house. The others are within 500 feet. I can see two of them from windows in her kitchen. The third takes up most of the view out of her living room windows. "They came onto our neighbor's property in August 2009, on a Saturday," Joyce recalled. She continued:

I was in the living room, working out on my elliptical. Through the window I saw trucks starting to show up, and I thought, that's odd. But they let people come over and fish out of their ponds, so it's not super odd. But they were more than what looked normal. And a few minutes later, my neighbor called me and he said "they're coming to put in a well, and there's nothing that I can do about it." And she told me, the wife told me, later, that the way that she found out that they're going to do that was: previously, there was a white pickup truck out there on their property, and she thought it was odd. So she went out to talk to them and she said "Do you want to fish?" Because lots of people come out and they want fish. I guess that's normal out here. They'll drive by and they'll see somebody's pond and they will go up and ask "Can we fish?" It's kind of the neighborly sort of thing. He was very apologetic, but he said "I'm sorry, ma'am, but I'm actually looking to see where I'm going to put my bulldozer." And she said "What bulldozer?" And he said "I'm sorry, we're . . . they're getting ready to put in a well here." So it was a subcontractor that told her!

I ask: "It's on her property? Someone just shows up to her property and says we're going to drill?"

Joyce nods. "It's like we're not even here."

Research Questions

Natural gas development has expanded across the United States in recent years. Natural gas is touted as a "greener alternative" to other fossil fuels, and developing this resource in order to reduce dependence on foreign oil is a significant component of U.S. energy policy. Yet this comes at a cost to local communities, which bear the brunt of associated pollution and inconvenience.

In this book I present a case study of natural-gas-development-related health activism in the urban areas of the Barnett Shale, the natural gas field (located in North Texas) that is furthest along in development of all such fields in the United States. I use field work, in-depth interviews, and document analysis collected during the course of a two-year ethnographic study to untangle the complexity of natural-gas-related activities occurring in urban environments.

My sociological account details the experiences and the meanings of activities related to natural gas development from the perspectives of people living with those activities—people who view urban gas development as

a significant threat to public health, and who, as a result, have (often reluctantly) become health activists.

This is a story about natural gas development in the Barnett Shale and
the impact it has had on North Texas. Specifically, I investigate what happened when a predominantly white, conservative, middle-class population
was suddenly exposed to the invasiveness of shale gas drilling in their
neighborhoods, and the largely political reasons that dangerous practice
has been allowed to continue. But it is more than that—it is a story of
the health of a community, of how members of a community respond to
perceived health threats, and about how people respond in the face of
fear of invisible toxins. It is a *sociology of community-level health threats*—a
theoretical framework for understanding how people collectively cope
with health threats at the community level. Although this story is
situated in the specific context of North Texas, it has broader implications,
and it offers insights into the turmoil that communities in sacrifice zones
undergo (Lerner 2012) and how meaning is made by residents of these
communities.

Gunter and Kroll-Smith (2007, 7) write about the need to understand
local environmental conflicts *because* of the interconnections between the
global and the local. "Communities," they explain, "are affected by technological, political, economic, and cultural developments that originate
beyond their borders." Social activists repeat the refrain "Think globally, act
locally." Communities do not exist in isolation (certainly not in the United
States); events are interconnected between regions. The local environment
is embedded in a larger, globalized social system.

Natural gas activities in North Texas are sociologically interesting
because, in contrast with many other gas fields, development in the Barnett
Shale is happening in urban areas. Drilling, hydraulic fracturing ("fracking"), and other extraction and transport activities happen in close proximity to homes, schools, and businesses. And because the Barnett Shale is one
of the most developed shales in the world, lessons from this region may be
helpful to communities beginning this process. Previously inaccessible natural gas shales have been identified not only across the United States but in
many other parts of the world. Shale gas has the potential to shift the global
energy economy away from the Middle East. Simultaneously, geopolitical
changes are clashing with pollution threats to the environment. With the
notable exception of coal mining, the burden of ecological devastation

wrought by the mining of fossil fuels has been borne largely by populations in lesser-developed countries—populations with little or no control over industry. In contrast, extraction of fossil fuels in middle-class communities results in great environmentalist backlash, insofar as the population has more social capital. People in such communities have more resources at their disposal, including both a legal system in place to protect their interests and an ethos of democratic participation. Indeed, as will be shown in this book, many of the people pushing back against natural gas development are exercising these rights and abilities for the first time.

Place is important to this story, as it is in a specific place that pollution and resultant health impacts occur. The search for genetic factors, infectious agents, and lifestyle variables, in combination with the transient nature of modern human existence (the ease of movement in geographic space), has largely divorced people's understanding of disease causality from the centrality of place. Early in the history of medicine, place and illness were not so distant. Disease was understood in the context of its connection to place (Nichols 2008). But today "the relationship between disease and place is often murky or lost entirely" (ibid., 64). Exposure to a certain toxic chemical a decade or more ago may be causing present-day illness. It is difficult to pinpoint those types of sources as time passes and more variables enter the equation. Yet when toxic pollutants contribute to illness in community members, place becomes an essential component in understanding cause and effect.

In her story of confronting an environmental threat to health, Nichols (ibid., 72) poignantly writes that "it is only through telling scientifically based, carefully crafted stories that place and disease can be reunited. In this context, even individual stories matter." This is precisely my aim in this book. I present a scientifically based story of natural gas drilling in North Texas and demonstrate how communities cope with threats to public health, and how place and disease are united.

National attention to health and pollution effects of natural gas development increased when development began in the Marcellus Shale, most of which is in the states of New York, Pennsylvania, and West Virginia. Goodell (2012) writes:

At first, when oil and gas producers confined themselves to fracking in the wide-open spaces of Texas and Oklahoma, nobody much gave a damn. The trouble started in 2007, when drilling operators made a run on the Marcellus Shale, a broad region of gas reserves that stretched through Pennsylvania and up into Ohio and New York.

Introduction 5

Almost overnight, fracking's technological miracle was recast as the next great environmental menace.

Natural gas drilling may have gained national attention when it threatened populations in the eastern U.S., but some folks did give a damn about activities in Texas and Oklahoma. Activists in Texas tried to get their voices heard, but it seemed that few listened until the water supplies for New York City were threatened by activities in the Marcellus Shale. Perhaps this was due to a misconception held by Goodell and others that gas drilling was confined to the "wide open spaces" of Texas. But that is inaccurate—much of the drilling in Texas is occurring in highly populated residential spaces.

Health activists in the Barnett Shale fight against their invisibility. They fight against stereotypes of Texas and a strong history of oil and gas culture in the state. They fight to protect the health and safety of their communities. In this book, I explore the relationship between the history and culture of oil and gas development in Texas and how that history bears on present-day anti-drilling activism. I present a picture of the activists themselves— who they are and how they came to be involved in this issue. I discuss the ways in which they protest and try to change the system, and the obstacles they encounter.

I also recount how activists engage in meaning making. I will demonstrate how they construct a social representation of natural gas drilling as a threat to community health and a cause of disease, and I will examine the challenges they face in that construction. The activists make meaning through discursive practice, and face many obstacles as they move from meaning making to action. I will discuss that ways in which their knowledge is questioned by the industry and by government regulators, and I will explore their quest for visibility in the gas fields.

Is natural gas development putting public health at risk? As I will show, natural gas activists have amassed considerable evidence to support such a claim, and they work to make others understand what it is like to live with gas development in the hope that they will no longer be invisible in the gas fields.

Theoretical Orientations

Social Representation Theory
"All research," Pascale writes (2011, 3), "is anchored to basic beliefs about how the world exists." This work is informed by a number of theoretical

orientations, lenses through which I understand social interaction and through which I examine the data I have collected. Most importantly, I draw on social representation theory to explore the process of meaning making. Social representation theory elucidates how people make sense of their worlds through shared understandings. It argues that people construct meaning about their worlds through social interaction. Creating meaning from interactions facilitates the creation of a collective understanding of an issue. This theoretical approach guided my initial questions about how people had come to frame natural gas drilling as an environmental health threat. I wanted to know what information they drew on, shared, or created to derive this conclusion. And once the conclusion was drawn, I wanted to explore the various ways in which they acted on that knowledge. As will be demonstrated, knowledge construction in this case was emergent from social interaction. This is an iterative spiral through micro-level and macro-level processes, creating and refining meaning, and solidifying the social representation of gas drilling in these communities. Through collective evaluation and integration of individual perceptions, a social understanding—consisting of agreed-upon meanings a group of people hold about a phenomenon—is created.

Durkheim (1912 [1995, 438]) was the first to write about how societies create collective representations of social constructs. He viewed collective representations as the embodiment of knowledge that a society holds about a particular social object:

Solely because society exists, there also exists beyond sensations and images a whole system of representations that possess marvelous properties. By means of them, men understand one another, and minds gain access to one another. They have a kind of force and moral authority by virtue of which they impose themselves upon individual minds. From then on, the individual realizes, at least dimly, that above his private representations there is a world of type-ideas according to which he had to regulate his own; he glimpses a whole intellectual world in which he participates but which is greater than he.

Agreed-upon meanings emerge through discursive practice—through social engagement as mediated in conversations, texts, images, and other collective communication. Durkheim (ibid., 437) wrote that collective representations "add to what our personal experience can teach us all the wisdom and science that has collectively massed over the centuries" and that "logical thought is possible only when man has managed to go beyond the fleeting representations he owes to sense experience and in the end to conceive a whole world of stable ideas, the common ground of intelligences."

Building on Durkheim's notion of collective representation, Moscovici (1963) proposed social representation theory to understand "common sense," or everyday knowledge. He sought to explain how people create social reality in their day-to-day lives. He conceptualized social representations as dynamic, created and re-created in the course of social interaction (Murray 2002). Of particular interest within social representation theory are the values, ideas, and practices that individuals draw upon both to establish social order and to facilitate communication. As members of a group interact, they construct and refine their representations. When new information is brought into the discourse, it is compared against the existing framework. If the new information fits the framework, it is integrated and may serve to shape the social representation. When new information is not compatible with existing frameworks, or when it is in conflict with existing frameworks, a new representation may emerge. This occurs through collective processing of information.

Social representations, Murray (2002, 668) notes, are "considered the defining characteristic of communities." Individuals are embedded in multi-layered communities, in intersectionalities of a myriad of social constructs. The level of involvement in a community may vary from person to person; however, community members engage as a group in an iterative process of creating and re-creating social representations.

Wundt (1916) characterized collective representations as "those mental products which are created by a community of human life and are, therefore, inexplicable in terms merely of individual consciousness, since they presuppose the reciprocal action of the many." Social representations are the means by which a social group influences individuals within it (Moscovici 1963; Riley and Baah-Odoom 2010). Social representations are guideposts for interpreting reality, and they influence behavior and values. Lived experience is not static, and people are continually, actively engaged in refining both meaning and being.

A social representation has two components: a core and a periphery (Moscovici 1963). The core is relatively stable. It creates meaning, and it places normative constraints on the individuals in the social group. The periphery is malleable. The periphery shifts with the accumulation of new information; however, it functions to maintain the stability of the core. At its core, a social representation carries certain socially constructed meanings, assumptions, and values. In the periphery we find an amalgam of variation; every derivation from the core social construct exists on and enriches this periphery.

Social representations are driven by discourse (Potter and Edwards 1999). Language provides meaning to social phenomena, and shapes human understanding of reality. This is a process of debate and counter-debate, a process of shared human interaction. The creation of social knowledge is a permeable, dialectic process, a dialogue between individuals and their environments.

This is not a neutral process, however. Social representations are shaped by power differentials (Foucault 1971 [1972]). Some members of the community will typically have more power to shape this discourse than others. They may have greater epistemic privilege—that is, their ways of knowing about the world may have more weight than those of others. They may have greater social capital—a greater ability to ensure that their voice is heard within the cacophony of voices, or greater control over the crafting of the discourse. The manner in which information is framed and processed benefits different factions of the social body. Words themselves construct and control collective representations. Language classifies and regulates bodies (Foucault 1961 [1965]). Deconstruction of discourse reveals underlying power relations because the emergent construction is shaped by the words used, and by who uses them.

Some scholars believe that the social representations a group holds are what define the group as a community (Murray 2002, 668). Individuals within the community process information about health threats collectively in an iterative, emergent process of creation and re-creation between members of the community. The engine of this process is discursive practice (Potter and Edwards 1999). Change is not a simple, linear process, but a non-linear spiral of debate and counter-debate. The creation of social knowledge is a permeable, dialectic process, a dialogue between and among individuals and their environments. Ultimately the created knowledge becomes part of a community's identity.

The Environment, Abstract and Concrete

Part of the emergent representation about natural gas drilling is grounded in the community's perceptions and understandings about the natural environment. Dating to the Enlightenment, the Cartesian duality of man and nature separated the two within philosophical thought and practice. Man (and I use the pronoun intentionally) was said to have dominion over the natural world. Western philosophical thought has historically viewed humanity as separate from and above nature, with nature divided from culture (a product of humans), as if humans were somehow outside of, or separate from, their surroundings. Dichotomies—man/woman, light/dark, human/animal, culture/nature—were ultimately read as positive/negative. Humans controlled nature, taking what was needed for human good and giving little or no thought to environmental impacts. Additionally, urbanization and industrialization drew humans out of their "natural" environments into human-created spaces. This was more than a philosophical problem: as humans spent increasing amounts of time dwelling in human-made environments, the natural world was increasingly forgotten.

Ultimately, however, human mastery over the earthly domain is a fantasy, as is evidenced particularly by natural and technological disasters. Positioning culture as superior to nature in our philosophical traditions negates the embeddedness of humanity in the material world. This is alarming in view of the very real environmental threats humanity now faces.

"For most Americans," Edelstein (2004, 81) writes, "environment is an abstract concept. It is a sphere of reality that is somehow separated from us and our lives. We know there are terrible problems with the environment, and we want them to be addressed, but we do not necessarily associate these problems with ourselves and our homes."

Industrialization and urbanization functionally removed humans from "the environment" and "created the impression that not only was the environment a source of inexhaustible natural resource, but also that humans could manipulate and control that environment to suit their needs" (Dunlap 2002, 332). This hubris led to the dismissal of environmental problems. According to Grebowicz and Merrick (2013, 31), "the ways in which we think, represent, and call upon nature is inherently political, with worldly consequences for the ways we live as humans, societies, and in relation to human and nonhuman others." Those consequences are being felt in many local communities.

For most people, however, the environment is a benign abstraction. It is "the view." Yet we are in fact embedded in that view. The transition of the environment from abstraction to objectification is illuminated abruptly when the view changes as a result of industrial signifiers entering previously unoccupied spaces. Shocked to attention, Edelstein writes (2003, 574), "victims are forced to recognize the vulnerability of natural systems and their intimate interconnectedness and interrelatedness with their surround, suddenly perceiving threats not previously in awareness. Environment is now central to their understanding of life."

Through the recognition of a health threat in the environment, the environment itself becomes concrete: as culture/nature dualisms collapse, we realize we are, in the words of Donna Haraway (in Grebowicz and Merrick 2013), elements within a "natureculture" assemblage.

My research is informed by both medical and environmental sociology. Whereas inquiry into the social aspects of health and medicine is well developed within sociology, environmental sociology (as a distinct field of study) is newer, having emerged in the 1970s. Before that time, in alignment with the emphasis in philosophy on culture as opposed to nature, sociologists paid little attention to the biophysical environments in which society was nested (Dunlap 2002). Early definitions of the field varied between explorations of environmental issues and explorations of the interaction of social structures and the environment.

Ethnography

"Long before there were statistics or scientific studies," Nichols writes (2008, 71), "there were stories—stories that warned of the link between environmental factors and their potential health effects." In sociological research, method should flow from theoretical orientation. A researcher should ask what the best technique is for collecting data that will inform the particular research questions under consideration. I approached this story ethnographically to better understand how communities recognize and cope with health threats. By immersing myself in the happenings, I wanted to understand the perspectives and points of view of health activists. Transparency of method was called for at the founding of ethnography by Malinowski (1922), and I believe researchers should be clear about how they conduct their work so that others can better evaluate their results. The ethnographic approach is one epistemology for understanding the social world, and is one that I embrace.

Ethnography involves the intentional, systematic collection of information and data on the lived realities of a particular group of people. As

Madden writes (2010, 32), "being with people (or more precisely, being ethnographic with people), in their time and space, in all their strangeness and in their mundane quotidian flow, is still one of the most valued ways to build a qualitative understanding of the particulars and generalities of the human condition."

Often referred to as "deep hanging out," ethnography involves sharing people's social space, engaging in shared activities, talking, observing, and eventually attempting to understand a slice of the social world (Westbrook 2008). The ethnography is a "storied reality" (ibid., 6), an "insider's depiction" (inasmuch as a researcher can understand the insider's perspective) supported with significant amounts of data and analysis (Charmaz 2006, 21). In this work, I seek to honor stories and narrative forms, and to value and embrace community organization for social change. These standpoints influence and permeate my work.

I embrace a feminist ethic of co-created knowledge, and I draw on eco-feminist writings to consider the impact of humans on the natural world and the power differentials that operate in such acts (Littig 2001). As my analysis will show, these power differentials may be read as both gendered and sexual. I embark on a self-referential, feminist reflexivity, considering the researcher as referent. I acknowledge my positionality as a researcher in the research process. As a feminist researcher, I continually interrogate my own subjectivity in relation to the object of inquiry. I believe such transparency is an important component of establishing the validity of this type of inquiry.

Ethnographic practice involves rich description to support one's findings, and a goal of constructing social theory (Madden 2010). Social theory is constructed recursively during the research process. Charmaz (2006, 10) writes: "Research participants' implicit meanings, experiential views—and researchers' finished grounded theories—are constructions of reality." As this research explores the social construction of natural gas drilling as a collective health threat, use of an ethnographic approach is instrumental both in theorizing the phenomenon and in suggesting practical solutions.

Data Collection

Most of the data for this project were collected in the field—in communities in the Barnett Shale where active natural gas development was under way. Fieldwork is an embodied practice (Madden 2010), a physical engagement of the researcher with the phenomena of inquiry. The field I worked in was multi-sited. As Westbrook writes (2008, 53), "contemporary ethnography tends to be multi-sited," and "the ethnographer must stage multiple conversations, with different subjects, positions (physically but especially socially) different from one another." Numerous individuals and organizations with various standpoints and agendas are involved in natural gas activism; it is a complex picture. There was not simply one field in which activities took place, but multiple, sometimes overlapping, spaces.

My primary data came from fieldwork and from in-depth interviews (typically lasting from one to three hours) with twenty key players in the debate about drilling in the Barnett Shale. These people are publicly identifiable as active in the protest of natural gas drilling in their communities. They regularly speak at public meetings. They produce reports for city officials and other entities. Most of them maintain blogs and/or Facebook groups dedicated to the opposition of drilling in the Barnett Shale. I also had the opportunity to interview some of the regulatory officials involved, both at the local level and at the state level.

I attended grassroots organizational meetings, "town hall" meetings hosted by regulatory agencies (such as the Environmental Protection Agency and the Texas Commission on Environmental Quality), meetings of municipal and county oil and gas task forces, and city council meetings. I attended and participated in protests and rallies. I had numerous informal, instrumental conversations with people at these events. I wrote detailed field notes after each meeting, event, or interview I participated in. In the field notes I worried less about what people were saying than about the actions that had happened, and I relied on digital recordings when transcribing what was said. I kept a running file of field notes and interspersed them with extensive memo writing.

I visited several sites with active natural gas drilling operations in order to better understand how the proximity of drilling might affect residents. One home I visited was in the center of three pad sites. Two of the sites were within 500 feet of the home, and a third was 200 feet from the home. One of the pads was fitted with a diesel-fueled compressor that ran 24 hours per day and made a loud clanging noise that could be heard inside the house.

Secondary data included news articles, reports generated by regulatory agencies, websites (including those from governmental and regulatory agencies and from grassroots organizations), scientific reports, blogs, and open-access online discussion groups. All the secondary data that I used are publicly available.

In addition, I draw on what St. Pierre (2011, 621) calls "transgressive data":

emotional data, dream data, sensual data, memory data, and *response data*—data that were not visible and that disrupted linearity, consciousness, and the mind/body dichotomy. Much data—*what we think when we think about a topic*—were identified *during* analysis and not before. Until one begins to think, one cannot know what one will think with. In that sense, data are collected during thinking and . . . especially during writing.

I gained entrée into the activist and regulatory groups by being a constant presence at meetings. I asked informal questions during the events and had informal conversations with people in attendance before and after the events. Over time I grew to know some of the major participants, who then introduced me to others. During formal interviews, I spoke with people in depth about their experiences, in a narrative fashion. Most of the interviews began with the simple question "Tell me your story, how did you get involved?" and then developed into participant-led discussions.

An ethnographer seeks to understand stories from the point of view of the participants, "intertwining action and consciousness, making the 'knower and known inseparable'" (Butler-Kisber 2010, 63). Narrative research—research through storytelling—explores how people make sense of the world, how events influence people, and how in turn, people affect the world. This technique hinges on the assumption that "knowledge generation . . . is spatial, temporal and selective[,] comes directly from perception of experience, and is socially constructed" (ibid., 65). Research method should always be informed by one's theoretical orientation, and choice of this method of study was directly informed by the theoretical orientation of social representation theory. This mode of inquiry links macro-level and micro-level social processes by considering the feedback between individuals and broader social forces (Gullion 2002).

By valuing narrative accounts, the researcher is confronted with the challenge of the "Rashomon Effect": the same event, viewed from different standpoints can result in very different accounts. The accounts in this volume are presented both from the perspectives of the people I interacted with and from my own perspective. Other actors in the events might express differing viewpoints. I suspect this would particularly be the case for persons affiliated with the industry and other pro-drilling voices. I would not be surprised at all if they expressed dissatisfaction with this tale of events. Indeed, capturing their perspective is a ripe area for further research.

In the course of ethnographic research, the researcher "lives the story" with the participant (Butler-Kisber 2010, 78) to the extent possible. This requires building trusting relationships with people and spending significant amounts of time interacting with participants in the field to develop understanding.

When acknowledging the multitude of standpoints, one might question the derived knowledge claims. Are they valid? What is the "truth" of the situation? Butler-Kisber (ibid., 78) writes correctly that critique of this type of research should focus on trustworthiness rather than generalizability, and on the plausibility and logic of the presentation rather than on an absolute truth (if such a thing even exists). In research of this sort, comprehensive evidence builds the case for the findings. Among the questions one must ask are these: Is the case made with quality evidence? Is the work comprehensive enough to draw conclusions? Is the argument coherent? Is it insightful? As a public sociologist, I would add another question: Does the work benefit society?

As I have already mentioned, as interviews were transcribed I kept detailed theoretical memos alongside the transcriptions. To facilitate triangulation, I collected multiple sources of data, then deconstructed these sources in order to reconstruct not only the course of events but plausible explanations for those events. Thousands of pages of text were analyzed.

Because of the large number of "facts" cited by all sides, constant comparison of the data was important. But it wasn't always possible to determine the source of the facts people repeated or to determine how "true" they were. This is not unusual in cases of contested science in an environmental controversy, and it emphasized to me the difficulties the participants felt when building their arguments.

The participants consented to my use of a digital recorder during all but one of the interviews. I placed the recorder on the table between us, always clearly visible. At public meetings, the recorder was placed on a table near the main speaker. Any public meeting that was recorded would have been one in which there would be no reasonable expectation of privacy. Often these meetings were videotaped by the agency hosting the meeting, and they were typically attended by several news reporters. Smaller, non-public meetings were not recorded; however, I wrote field notes after such meetings.

Though I was somewhat concerned about the obtrusiveness of the digital recorder and whether having it in sight would alter people's discussions, I took heart from Duneier (1999, 340), who noted that "the [Howard] Becker principle comes into play: most social processes are so organized that the presence of a tape recorder . . . is not as influential as all the other pressures, obligations, and possible sanctions in the setting."

All of the formal interviews were conducted with the expectation of privacy, and therefore I do not use any of the interviewee's names in this book. The names that appear in the vignettes that begin many of the chapters have been changed, as have identifying characteristics. When discussing data obtained from public sources, such as public presentations, published news reports, or blogs that identify an author, I do use people's real names or cite the source in the references. Many of the activists have made names for themselves as public spokespersons. Some have built careers on their activism and should be recognized activists. In addition, this practice, as Duneier (1999) noted, allows their voices to come through in a way that also keeps me as the researcher accountable for my interpretations.

With the exception of the interviews, all the data were collected in settings open to the general public—settings in which there would be no reasonable expectation of privacy. Nonetheless, to the extent possible, I identified and reasserted my role as a researcher, to ensure that no covert behavior was taking place on my part.

Trust and motive proved to be significant themes throughout the study. I was asked on several occasions who was funding my project. (It was not funded.) At times I questioned the motives of the people around me. Though they initially appeared to be opposed to drilling, some of the individuals I encountered turned out to be involved in this issue for profit rather than altruism. The natural gas controversy created a market opportunity for them—for example, an opportunity to serve as paid environmental consultants. Some of the people involved were trying to make names for themselves, either as professional environmentalists or as future professional environmentalists, and were actively promoting their blogs or their research. Some, like me, were motivated by career aspirations. (I must be honest and note that, although this issue is important to me personally, writing this book also supports my academic goals.) And some of the people involved in these activities, I discovered, were "plants"—public relations professionals posing as independent, pro-development activists. This was another reason to engage in constant comparison of the data. Many of the "facts" presented to me required extensive validation.

To protect privacy even further, throughout this work I have omitted the names of specific gas companies that I encountered. I have done this not to protect the companies, but to protect respondents from possible breaches of privacy or acts of retaliation. I've also removed specific city names when knowledge of the city could reveal the identity of any of the respondents.

The events discussed in this book provide a snapshot of activities that continue to unfold. I started this project during the summer of 2011 and continued data collection and analysis through May of 2013. Although such a project is necessarily bounded by time, I believe it is important to note that the process of forming a social representation of natural gas drilling in the Barnett Shale is ongoing. Activists in the Barnett Shale continue to fight for the health and safety of their communities.

Grounded Theory

I used a grounded approach to data analysis. Grounded methods take an inductive approach to reasoning, and social theory emerges during the course of analysis and collection of data. This is a dialectical process "in which data collection and analysis reciprocally inform and shape each other through an emergent iterative process" (Charmaz 2011, 360). Charmaz writes that this approach "(1) rejects claims of objectivity, (2) locates researcher's generalizations, (3) considers researchers' and participants' relative positions and standpoints, (4) emphasizes reflexivity, (5) adopts sensitizing concepts such as power, privilege, equity, and oppression, and (6) remains alert to variation and difference."

In my project, as in many other grounded projects, data collection and analysis occurred simultaneously, informing one another during the research process. "By asking analytic questions during each step in the iterative process," Charmaz writes (ibid., 361), "the researcher raises the abstract level of analysis and intensifies its power."

Duneier (2012) argues that researchers using a grounded approach should put their data on trial. To do so, I compared data with other data along each step in the process. As the research progressed, analytic categories emerged and were refined. I tried to look beyond my own interpretations of events to glean meanings as perceived by the participants, simultaneously considering the bulk of the data rather than any one participant's interpretation of events. This involved not only continual reexamination of the data, but also reentry into the field for clarification as themes emerged.

Early in the project, the coding of data was necessarily broad, and it led to themes and categories of interest. Once these themes and categories were recognized within the data, I conducted theoretical sampling of the data to round out the theme or category. In some cases, I found that an identified category was not robust but that other categories were well supported among the data types. As categories developed, I identified relationships and hierarchies between and among them that helped me to flesh out my theorizing.

Reflexivity

Addressing issues of methodological reflexivity has become a hallmark of ethnography (Madden 2010). I work at the intersection of science and art, where the two overlap, through the use of systematic, established sociological method and creative presentation (Gullion 2014). This interrogative space lends itself to the imaginative theory construction that is the goal of ethnographic practice.

I became interested in the health effects of natural gas drilling in urban settings a few years before beginning this project. I live and work in the Barnett Shale, one of the most productive natural gas fields in the world. When I first noticed the erection of "Christmas trees" in nearby neighborhoods, I was the Chief Epidemiologist of the Denton County Health Department. ("Christmas tree" is jargon for the assembly of control valves, pressure gauges, and chokes at the top of a gas well.) In the course of my job, I occasionally fielded complaints about the wells. People would call and say that they were getting headaches from the fumes, or that the noise was causing them stress that exacerbated their diabetes, or that they had developed neurological or other symptoms from their exposure to the wells. I heard enough complaints to raise some alarm, and I began to follow local news accounts of drilling activities. I was paid via a state-funded grant to be an

infectious disease epidemiologist, and environmental health was outside of
my purview. There was little I could do to respond to these complaints aside
from referring people to the appropriate regulatory agency. In addition, at
that time the county's environmental health program had only three
employees, and they were tasked primarily with monitoring septic systems
in unincorporated areas and with inspecting public school cafeterias for
schools outside of cities. They did not have enough time, funding, expertise, or legal authority to follow up on health complaints related to natural
gas drilling.

In 2010 I left the Denton County Health Department and joined the
sociology faculty at Texas Woman's University. In the summer of 2011, I
officially began the study that led to the writing of this book.

The first interview I conducted was with a woman with whom I had
worked previously on an unrelated issue. Remembering that she had started
an organization to protest natural gas drilling in her neighborhood, I contacted her for the purpose of setting up an interview. The interview lasted
more than three hours. At the conclusion, she gave me a list of names of
other activists she thought I should contact.

Later that summer, I attended a meeting that the Texas Commission on
Environmental Quality (TCEQ) hosted for the purpose of getting feedback
from citizens on its revised plan to bring the Dallas–Fort Worth metroplex
into compliance with the U.S. Environmental Protection Agency's standards for air quality. Before that meeting, two environmental activist organizations staged a rally outside the government building in which the
meeting was being held (in 105-degree heat) to specifically protest natural
gas development as a cause of the region's air-quality problems. The activists from the rally and others then testified at the hearing. The testimony
was transcribed by a court reporter and later made publicly available on the
TCEQ's website. (This turned out to be a norm of many government-hosted
meetings, and I used the transcriptions as a data source.) At that meeting, I
handed out a number of fliers inviting activists to contact me if they were
interested in being interviewed. Many did.

From that point on, I worked to become a fixture at meetings of activists
concerned with gas drilling in the area. Because of the size of the Dallas–
Fort Worth metroplex (which has a population of about 7 million), and
because of the size of the Barnett Shale (5,000 square miles), I focused on
activists in Denton County and Tarrant County, the so-called core locations

for urban drilling. These were the activists I came to know the best; how-ever, it is notable that many of the activists travel to one another's meet-ings. Thus, at a meeting held in the city of Denton, I would see activists from neighboring cities, including Dallas and Fort Worth. I focused my efforts on those activists and their activities. In doing so, I may have left out activists who are quite vocal and visible in other geographic areas of the Barnett Shale.

I live on the boundary between scientist and community member, and that is reflected in my work. Conducting ethnographic research "at home" is an accepted practice, and it presents both opportunities and chal-lenges (Lal 1999; Madden 2010). Researching in one's usual lived environ-ment, one must look—and see—what has always been there but may not have been noticed. In the settings in which I conducted my research (all of which were open to the general public), I vacillated between pure observer and participant observer. I did not offer my own opinion unless asked directly; however, I did ask questions as they occurred to me, just as any other meeting participant might have. Likewise, I found myself moving between the spaces of objective researcher and community member who is personally concerned about threats to her family's health. This issue was raised directly for me in a meeting in which I learned that a well would be drilled and fracked within two blocks of my children's school. At that moment, my scientific objectivity about the meeting was superseded by my role as a participant and a mother with questions about the safety of that site.

Aside from a general interest in health activism, I had did not have a defined research question when I began my work. This proved challenging for me when I had to explain my research in its early stages, but it allowed for what I believe are rich post-analysis findings. I was able to immerse myself in events with few preconceptions and to remain open to what was happening around me.

A Note on Research Ethics

Ethnography requires the researcher to form relationships with the people involved in the study. The researcher gets to know the participants and works to build mutually trusting relationships with them. At the same time, the researcher must be cognizant of the boundaries between researcher and researched and of the power dynamics that are involved in research. As Madden (2010) notes, the researcher should be "close, but not too close" to the participants and their activities. I grappled with this boundary at several points during the research.

As I spent more and more time in the field, I formed friendships with some of the people involved. Or did I? I went to lunch with one activist who I'd come to consider a friend. She began to hug me, then said "Wait, can I hug you if I'm one of your specimens?" We laughed about this and hugged, but the statement, while humorous, was an acknowledgment that ours was a friendship predicated on purposes—mine to conduct an ethnographic study, hers to get her story heard. The question was also a reflection of the power dynamics between us. A subject's calling herself a "specimen" brought to mind a laboratory setting, with experiments conducted on objects—a kind of dehumanization that I wanted to avoid.

I also experienced role discomfort during the rewriting of one city's oil and gas ordinance. A grassroots organization was unhappy with a draft of the ordinance proposed by city officials. During a large open meeting which the public was invited to attend, the membership of the organization decided to rewrite the ordinance, section by section, then to present their results to the city council. A listserv was set up, and the members began the intensive process of reworking the ordinance (which would have to be submitted to the city council in a very short time period). This was a tremendous undertaking, particularly for citizen volunteers doing it in their free time.

I had been invited to join the group because of my expertise in public health, and I was asked to contribute to the rewriting process. I grappled with my role. How much of a participant should I be? Should I help rewrite a city ordinance? Feeling that too much participation would be too unobjective, I decided to step back from the process and let the other members (all of whom were highly capable) work out the text. Did I make the right choice? I now believe I did, but I struggled with it at the time. Was I taking and not giving enough back?

My struggle became the center of discussion one evening in my graduate course on qualitative research methods. I told my students I was reminded of *Star Trek*'s Prime Directive: that there should be no interference with the social development of another society. In all honesty, I hadn't been sure that I could contribute much to the rewriting of the ordinance. Though I understood much about natural gas development and the associated toxicology, I was uncertain whether I should or could translate that knowledge into public policy. Though I could have advised the policy makers, I wasn't sure that it was in my purview to write policy. In addition, I thought it would be arrogant for me to assume that I knew more than the activists—they had become experts on this topic, whereas I was an observer (a knowledgeable, informed observer, but still an outsider).

My decision drew criticism from a member of the group who felt I should take a more activist approach. I do believe one can be an academic activist, however. My own activism is expressed by this volume. I reasserted my specific role as a sociological researcher with the goal of obtaining, processing, and compiling the very information that the activists and groups with whom I interacted wanted to make public.

Overview of Chapters

I begin chapter 1 with an overview of oil and gas development. I discuss oil and gas culture in Texas and provide a brief history of mineral extraction in the state. I also discuss the historical geopolitical climate surrounding the use of fossil fuels and how natural gas influences global economics. This history helps to explain some of the ongoing conflicts between citizens, governmental regulators, and the oil and gas industry.

In chapter 2, I examine the physical processes of natural gas development, extraction, and transport. I discuss hydraulic fracturing ("fracking") of gas wells, the issues associated with fracking, and other stages in the process of drilling for natural gas. Insofar as these activities take place in urban, largely residential areas in much of the Barnett Shale, illuminating their technical aspects also illuminates the sources of citizens' complaints. Natural gas activities are industrial in nature, and the physical placement of industry in residential zones can be quite disruptive and disconcerting for the residents.

The overview extends into chapter 3, in which I draw on the literature on possible human health concerns associated with natural gas extraction activities and on personal accounts from participants in the study. In that chapter, I explore air, water, and soil contamination associated with the natural gas industry; I also discuss research on cancer clusters, as they play an important role in the narrative of gas extraction.

In chapter 4, I review the legal and regulatory issues associated with natural gas development. I discuss the legal quagmire between mineral rights and surface rights. I also discuss the fragmentation of regulatory agencies in Texas and its implications for communities undergoing gas development. I explore the approaches of three different North Texas communities in coping with natural gas extraction as a perceived health threat, the use of talismans (social objects that are imbued—rightly or wrongly—with the perceived ability to protect the citizenry from negative health effects), and issues of environmental justice (particularly in relation to mining).

In chapter 5, I discuss "reluctant activists"—members of the community who were pushed or pulled into the natural gas drama. I integrate my findings into the literature on environmental justice. I complete this chapter with what I believe to be the end result of the fragmentation and contestedness of response to citizens' concerns: violence and intimidation against those who speak out against the industry.

In chapter 6, I consider how epistemic privilege shapes the public discourse about the health effects and the safety of natural gas development. I consider whose knowledge is legitimized and given credence in the discourse on natural gas extraction. I draw upon theories that discuss the role of expert science in nature and society. I consider how scientific uncertainty affects community-level decision making, and I critically evaluate issues of power and privilege related to the discursive practices surrounding natural gas development. I then turn specifically to the issue of "facts"— including their contested nature in the discourse on natural gas extraction and the tension between professional science and lay science in this scenario.

In chapter 7, I consider protest and the performance of pain. I specifically examine the construction of the protest narrative of natural gas extraction. I examine embodied storytelling as a discursive practice. I present toxic tours as instances of the performance of pain, and I situate such performances both in the literature on contaminated communities and specific instances in the Barnett Shale.

In chapter 8, I review the major findings of the study and present an emergent theory of community-level health threats, using natural gas extraction as a case study. I discuss the various components and characteristics of this theory and propose alternate scenarios in which this theory might be used.

The narrative of natural gas extraction is dynamic and ongoing. Although the location of my case study was North Texas, similar scenarios are unfolding across the United States. All data presented in this volume were current as of the time of writing; however, the story continues to evolve.

Most work on the sociological implications of oil and gas extraction centers on the "oil boom" towns that emerged when oil and gas operations moved quickly into rural areas with low population density. In oil boom towns, trucks, equipment, and personnel are brought in with seemingly little notice, and an infrastructure is erected quickly, sometimes haphazardly, only to be abandoned when the company is finished extracting the oil. Development per se is not as much of an issue in urban settings as it is in rural ones. In urban landscapes, businesses, neighborhoods, schools, and other signifiers of urban activity are already in place, and the oil and gas activities are inserted into spaces in the existing framework—for example, a 200-foot-tall drill appears one day behind backyard fences, squeezed into green spaces behind the homes. Hundreds of diesel trucks travel back and forth along a narrow two lane residential road that was never designed to maintain the continued stress. Pipes are laid across the back side of a soccer field. A parent notices her children are having a lot of bloody noses. Her neighbor observes the same in her own children. They look at the rig behind their fences and wonder if that is the cause. They talk to other neighbors, and soon the community is presented with a question: Is this a threat to our health?

1   Oil and Gas Development

Below the Texas soil lies a lively materiality—energy trapped in fossil form.

Between 300 million and 250 million years ago, in the Permian Period, the land mass that is now Texas was covered with a shallow sea. Organic matter drifted and accumulated on the sea floor, thickening into sediment. The sediment amassed and compressed into geological strata, an underground geological history. Through a fortuitous combination of bacteria, heat, and pressure, the layers transmorphied into black, liquid gold, which then remained sealed away until it was tapped to satisfy the needs created by proliferation of the automobile. It became one of the largest oil and gas fields the world would ever know.

No one paid much attention to the black viscous substance at first. Crude oil seeped up through the ground here and there, but since there was no real use for it, it was largely ignored. Occasionally cowboys discovered they could light puddles of it on fire and use them for heat or for cooking. When people discovered that the substance made for a good lubricant, they used it as axle grease. The first rudimentary oil well, called an "oil mine" (Cox 2012), was constructed in 1859 for the purpose of extracting oil to sell as a remedy for rheumatism (Horlacher 1929).

The discovery of kerosene changed the outlook for the substance. Kerosene was extracted from crude oil, and replaced whale oil and candlelight as the fuel of choice in lamps in the late 1880s, creating a new market for oil. Gasoline was a by-product of kerosene with no practical use at the time. It was often dumped in waterways for disposal (Mangan 1977, 35). Meanwhile, natural gas was discovered in 1821 in New York, with a hiss from a water well, and by the early 1900s, natural gas was also used to light the darkness.

But then everything changed for this viscous substance. The development of the automobile spawned the oil and gas industry. In 1886, Karl Benz invented a motorized carriage that would be the basis for modern transportation. The 1900s witnessed the emergence of the automobile, and within ten years more than half a million cars were on the road in the United States. In response, gasoline stations were constructed along the roadways to sell fuel to drivers. By the early 1920s, more than 20 million cars were on U.S. roads, and the Age of the Automobile was in full swing.

Another age was born along with it, an age of fossil fuel. The first major producing oil well was struck in 1901 near Beaumont, Texas. It was called Spindletop, and it produced more than 75,000 barrels of oil per day (Cox 2012). "The discovery," Cox writes (ibid., 1), "brought a tidal wave of money-hungry humanity to the upper Texas coast, the 1849 California gold rush all over again. But this time the gold was viscous and black. The Texas oil industry had begun in earnest, and neither Texas nor the world would be the same."

Texas Oil and Gas Culture

Oil and gas fields are the stuff of Texas legend. Picture fields of wells, and pump jacks bobbing up and down. On the drive from central Texas through west Texas, you will see hundreds of them out your window. More than one pump jack has been painted to resemble a grasshopper. The locals call West Texas "Big Sky Country." The land is flat, red clay dirt as far you can see in any direction. Scrub brush trees. No buildings, no mountains. Little farming here save for cotton. During harvest time, white fluffs drift across the highway. Towns are small, few, and far between, and the sky could swallow you whole. This is the Texas of imagination. Of the cowboy. Of the western frontier.

Texas oil culture can be traced to the oil boom of the 1930s. While the rest of the country was embroiled in the depths of the Great Depression, the oil men chased their fortunes in the Texas fields. In the early part of the twentieth century, as oil men rushed to Texas in pursuit of riches, they erected entire towns to support their search. Company towns. Boom towns. Towns designed specifically to meet the living needs of the men who worked the oil fields. According to Horlacher (1929, 21), who wrote about his experiences working the Texas oil fields in the 1920s, "it was a motley crowd, and they lived in all sorts of styles and manners—in tents, in the rudest of shacks, in more pretentious shacks, and in permanent abodes." Haphazardly constructed and a magnet for vice, the boom towns, as described by Mangan (1977, 23), were towns "whose breath reeked with bootleg whiskey and sulphurous gas."

Being an oil man was shrouded in romance. An oil man was a rugged adventurer, a cowboy, a wrangler. "We're living every kid's dream," Goodwyn (1996, 197) quotes one oil man as having said. "I'm looking for buried treasure. I'm the luckiest guy on earth." The oil man was part of a narrative of the beauty of strength, of taming the wilds, of conquering nature herself. His was a character in a proving ground for men, a world of hypermasculinity (or at least framed as such in the discourse of the time). "These unusual men, called Wildcatters," Mangan writes (1977, 16), "gambled everything in their search for liquid gold in unproven territory." According to Clark (1955, x), "great oil fields, as all other grand discoveries and inventions of progress, are usually found beyond the boundaries of comfortable knowledge and expert opinion in a realm inhabited by the Wildcatter." He who would tame the land was untamed himself, a force of nature all his own. "When East Texas boomed onto the oil scene in 1930," Clark writes (ibid., 2), "it had its chance to wreck the industry completely or to change it for the better. By will and determination, strong men in the face of chaos, confusion, adversity . . . were able to turn the field into the greatest force of good American industry has ever known."

Horlacher (1929, 23) writes of the thrill generated during exploratory drilling: "This new well . . . was what is known in the oil fraternity as a 'wild cat' or 'discovery' well. As such a well has a strong flow of oil, it is called a 'gusher' and as the possible profits are great it always created considerable excitement." Thrill of watching that liquid gold gush, thrill of accumulating profit.

Regulating the Black Giant

The romance of the Texas oil man had a dark side, however, one missing from the adventurous narrative. Though many fortunes have been made in the Texas oil and gas fields, Texans have also suffered from the burdens associated with cheap energy. Harsh working conditions, influxes of social problems, pollution, explosions—the reality of the oil and gas fields is far from glamorous. Margonelli (2007, 88) writes:

Whatever I pay for energy, I'll never pay as much as residents of Texas do. It's Texans who give up their backyards to noisy drilling rigs, their water to possible contamination by drilling; who breathe the air near the refineries of the Gulf Coast. When oil prices fall and people are thrown out of work, they're usually Texans. And whatever benefits the average Texan has received from the state's romance with oil, they're sacrificed mightily . . . and without much choice in the matter.

The wildcat drilling of the Texas oil boom generated a slew of social, environmental, and economic problems. "Drilling was brutally hard work, not to mention dangerous," Cox writes (2012, 15). "The state and federal governments had no industrial safety standards, and accidents, sometimes fatal and often debilitating, occurred frequently during the early days of Texas oil."

And there were problems other than the brutal working conditions in the boom towns. Horlacher witnessed gambling, fighting, and excessive drinking. "So many men had come to the oil fields," he writes (1929, 51), "that of course there was some lawlessness; in fact, at times, there was so much of it that the local police and the sheriff were unable to cope with it." These problems often followed the workers home. Writings of this time are notably lacking in women's perspectives, but women were certainly present. According to Horlacher (ibid., 53), "domestic life in the oil fields lacked much of being ideal. Husbands and wives seemed to have many difficulties, more it would seem than necessary. Life was rather lonesome for the women. . . . In fact, the situation looked rather hopeless to them and they seemed to lose interest in their homes and their husbands; nor did the men seem to take much pride in their homes or families." Many couples separated. Domestic violence was common, and "Often there were fights. Some of the men when they were drunk, beat up their wives." (ibid., 54)

Crime spun out of control in the boom towns. According to Clark (1955, 13), "local law enforcement officers were unable to handle the criminal element. Riot and insurrection were feared. Shootings and holdups were becoming commonplace. The state and federal liquor laws were flaunted in the faces of the citizens. Gambling was out in the open and it was impossible for the limited local authorities to cope with the dangers."

Along with the working conditions and the social problems came another problem of greed: there was too much oil drilling. Individual profits were based on getting the oil out of the ground, but so many people seeking their fortunes meant more wells were drilled than the market needed. Cost and price stabilization of energy have long been a political quagmire. The wildcatting days of the Texas oil boom quickly encountered a problem being faced again today by the natural gas companies: A glut of drilling leads to a glut in product, which results in falling prices. This led many in the Texas government to call for resource conservation.

"As frenzied activity mounted it became apparent that some controls would have to be established," Clark (1955, 11) writes, but "as soon as this intention became known, a great opposition sprang up. Landowners, businessmen, and other citizens were led to believe that controls would rob them of their great new wealth."

Throughout the history of oil and gas development there has been tension between the industry and government regulators. Many of the oil men perceived that the regulators stood in the way of profit, and the 1930s were marked by strife between new attempts at regulation and control of law and order, and the profit-seeking motives of the industry, "It was a day in which respect for the law had degenerated," Clark (1955, 11) writes. "Those people had no regard for the industry and certainly none for the laws of conservation. They were fly-by-night, get-rich-quick racketeers who saw their chance and took it." Never mind the mess in their wake.

Meanwhile, as Margonelli (2007, 92) notes, "to limit oil production to stabilize both the price and the pressure in the reservoir ... was un-American, uncapitalist, and utterly anti-oil. . . . It took the Texas Rangers, the National Guard, and a Supreme Court ruling finally to determine that shutting in production (or pro-rationing) was something the state Railroad Commission had the power to enforce." Price controls effectively saved the industry at the time by ensuring that while the commodity was still cheap, it was not *too cheap* to harm the oil companies.

Authority for regulation fell to the Texas Railroad Commission. Founded in 1891, the Railroad Commission was originally tasked with regulation of the haphazardly developing railroads. As with many other new industries, the railroads initially operated with a laissez-faire system of minimal governmental interference. The industry was highly competitive, yet was influenced by support from the government. The government encouraged growth, but problems quickly surfaced. Tracks were not standardized, which resulted in inabilities to connect lines. The railroads were plagued with poor service, corruption, and arrogance. Rates varied for transit, and the American public grew increasingly frustrated with the industry. "To many Americans," Childs writes (2005, 22), "the railways were monopolies that controlled the nation's economic development." State lawmakers finally intervened and created regulatory agencies to solve some of these troubles. And for a while, this is what the Texas Railroad Commission was tasked to do. It promoted expansion of the railways across the state, which contributed to economic growth.

With the discovery of large reserves of crude oil came a need to transport it to refineries and for sale. "Because oil does not stay in one place and because it must be transported over long distances," Childs writes (2005, 147), "policy makers had to adapt old land-use and transport laws to the new energy source." Enter the Texas Railroad Commission. While most oil and gas are transported by pipelines today, in the 1930s the industry relied on the railroad system for transport. Eventually, "pipelines replaced the railways but were able to do so only when the technology was developed and only when the government granted rights-of-way, a time-consuming process that added to the cost of doing business" (ibid., 149). As mentioned earlier, an added concern from the perspective on the part of the public was conservation. Here was this bountiful energy source that many did not wish to squander. Indeed, during the winter of 1917–18, Texans experienced coal and gas shortages, and many Texans suffered with little access to heat. Meanwhile, there were no price controls on oil and gas, and overproduction and wasteful practices inevitably led to falling profits.

Because of the need for railway transport, state lawmakers decided to give regulatory powers over the oil and gas industry to the Railroad Commission. It wasn't long before the Commission was caught in an imbroglio of politics: inter-agency disputes, state politics, and special interest groups all sought to influence the workings of the Commission. The agency became characterized by "a broader, personality-based leadership pattern" (Childs 2005, 170). This pattern continues to this day.

In 1931, the Railroad Commission began to institute limits on oil production in an attempt to control dropping prices (Clark 1955). Those limits were largely ignored by the producers. Conflicts increased between the developers and the government. Lawlessness in general permeated the boom towns, and the Railroad Commission, a small agency with fewer than thirty employees, had no real power to enforce its rules. In response, Governor Ross Sterling declared martial law and sent in the National Guard to impose order and to temporarily stop oil production. Twelve hundred National Guardsmen were dispatched to East Texas in an attempt to gain control over the situation.

The courts sided with the industry, and threw out many of the Railroad Commission's attempts at regulation. "Hot" (that is, illegal) oil thwarted attempts at limiting production, and the Texas Rangers were brought in to assist the Railroad Commission with enforcement. The federal court ruled the governor did not have the authority to take these sorts of law enforcement actions. Eventually the Supreme Court intervened (*Champlin Refg. Co. v. Oklahoma Corp. Commission* 1932), ruling it allowable for regulators to institute limits on the numbers of barrels produced, and some semblance of control was taken.

From the 1930s through the 1960s, the Railroad Commission maintained its tenuous function of regulating the supply of oil to the market (a role that was later assumed by OPEC). "The Railroad Commission . . . survived years of struggle, confrontations, and violence and saved the Texas oil industry from itself, at the same time setting standards for regulatory agencies everywhere," Walraven and Walraven note (2005, 114). Nonetheless, tension between the industry and regulators runs high even today.

Despite this history, the romance of the oil boom has remained a part of Texas culture. "The oil industry shaped the world's perception of Texas," Cox writes (2012, ix). "The wheeler-dealer type became a Texas icon, right up there with the cowboy."

Texans do not all ride horses. We do not all wear cowboy boots and listen to country music. We are not all "rednecks." And most of us do not own oil wells.

Rural or urban, Texans tend to be proud of their heritage. Bumper stickers such as "God invited me into heaven, but I chose Texas instead" and "I wasn't born a Texan, but I got here as soon as I could" are common. Our state flag flies level to the American flag. Television and radio spots remind us "Don't Mess with Texas" and that "We've got a culture all our own."

"I'm from Texas," one of the activists I spoke with said. "My family has oil and gas in East Texas. My family came from that. I understand its history. If you understand the history of oil and gas in this state, it's interesting. I mean everybody in this state, if they grew up here, has some connection to this industry. They've either worked for it or they had family in it."

Texas long dominated world oil production, but its production peaked in 1972 (Margonelli 2007). After a second, smaller boom in the 1980s, the major oil companies largely pulled out of the state, leaving for richer fields overseas. Most of the "old money" in Texas can be traced to the oil boom of the 1930s; much of the "new money" was derived from natural gas.

Another activist I spoke with told me: "I grew up in Corpus Christi. My mom always said, you need to be grateful because our city is funded by oil and gas money." Corpus Christi is a large port city. International cargo ships carry crude oil into the U.S. through Corpus Christi Bay, and a large industrial area processes and refines minerals.

In the course of my project, I identified several members of my own extended family with careers connected to the oil and gas industry, including one former roughneck and a petroleum engineer.

Energy in the United States

It is an understatement to say that the United States is dependent on fossil fuels. Rather, we are, in the words of George W. Bush, "addicted to oil." Yet there is a problem. The oil fields we have come to rely on are running dry. Most of our oil comes from the politically unstable Middle East. While on the campaign trail in 2008, Barack Obama noted that "our addiction to fossil fuels is one of the most serious threats to our national security" (cited in Klare 2012, 15). Saudi Arabia struggles to meet our demand (Deffeyes 2005). And many Americans agree that the United States' interventions in Afghanistan and Iraq are less about terrorism than about oil.

Geographically, the Middle Eastern oil fields are small. Together those oil fields account for less than 0.1 percent of the world's land area, and one could fit all of the Middle Eastern oil fields in the north-central region of the United States (Deffeyes 2005). Yet more than 25 percent of the oil produced in the world comes from the Middle East.

More than half of the oil consumed by the United States is imported. Although the U.S. has a significant number of producing oil fields, their production is low in comparison with oil fields in other parts of the world. (See table 1.1.)

Table 1.1

Major oil production.

	Production (million barrels per day)	Producing wells
Saudi Arabia	7.7	1,560
Russia	7.4	41,192
United States	5.8	521,070

source: Deffeyes 2005, 18

Hubbert's Peak is an estimate of peak world oil production. The geophysicist M. King Hubbert estimated in 1956 that the peak would be reached in the year 2000. Other scientists have placed the peak in the early to mid 2000s. Many experts argue that we are on the downward slope of that peak—that oil production is declining and will continue to do so (Deffeyes 2005). Meanwhile, worldwide demand for oil is increasing. "The issue," according to Goodell (2007, xiv), "is not simply that there are more people in the world, consuming more fossil fuels, but that as economies grow and people in developing nations are lifted out of poverty, they buy cars and refrigerators and develop an appetite for gas, oil, and coal. Between 1950 and 2000, as the world population grew by roughly 140 percent, fossil fuel consumption increased by almost 400 percent . . . . Of course every barrel of oil we pump out of the ground, every cubic foot of natural gas we consume, and every ton of coal we burn further depletes reserves."

The supplies of fossil fuels are finite. This fact, coupled with profit, makes for global power struggles. "Too many people define the U.S. problem as the amount of oil we import from the Middle East," Deffeyes writes (2005, 180). "They are missing the point. Most of Venezuela's and Mexico's oil exports come to the United States. North Africa ships oil to Europe. Middle Eastern oil moves largely to Japan and Europe. Export-import patterns can be rearranged with a few phone calls. As the world oil shortage becomes more severe, who ships what oil where is less relevant."

To address these issues, current U.S. energy policy encourages development of domestic energy sources. Prominent among these is the use of natural gas. The U.S. has an abundance of natural gas. The U.S. Geological Survey estimates the amount of recoverable natural gas within U.S. shales at approximately 200 trillion cubic feet (Andrews, Folger, and Humphries 2009). Thanks to new developments in drilling and extraction, we are able to utilize these resources to an extent never before realized.

Table 1.2
Annual energy generation in the United States.

Power source	Kilowatt-hours
Coal	1,968 billion
Nuclear	752 billion
Natural gas	612 billion
Hydroelectric	273 billion
Oil	109 billion
Other (including wind and geothermal)	84 billion

source: Deffeyes 2005, 57

Concerns over political instability in oil-rich nations and a dwindling oil supply are accompanied by a very real concern about pollution and its effects on the global climate. While the vast majority of automobiles are gasoline powered, in the U.S. most electricity is still generated by burning coal, which is highly polluting. (See table 1.2.) There is a great need for less polluting energy sources, and moves to "greener" alternatives are in progress.

Alternative fuel sources meet the needs for domestic energy production, a plentiful supply of energy resources, and reduced toxic burden. Natural gas has been hailed as the darling of alternative fuels, a "cleaner-burning" (i.e., less polluting) fuel, a "bridge fuel" to tide us over until greener sources, such as solar, wind, or geothermal, can be further developed. Natural gas has come to the dominant position of America's fuel of choice. Use of natural gas has increased by about 40 percent since 1977 (Goodell 2007, xv), and we now consume about 60 billion cubic feet of natural gas per day. It takes about 6,000 cubic feet of natural gas to equal the energy content of one barrel of oil. Of this amount, 24 percent is used to generate electricity in power plants, 35 percent goes to industrial uses, 16 percent is used for commercial heating, and 25 percent is used in residential heating (Deffeyes 2005, 57). And by-products from natural gas production are used to create an astonishing array of products, including plastics, fibers, pesticides, coatings, and solvents (ibid., 6).

"The major oil companies are not saying publicly that the oil game is over," writes Deffeyes (ibid., xvi). "If there were attractive prospects available, companies would be clawing their way over one another to get the drilling rights." But there is one area that companies are clawing at—unconventional natural gas drilling in shales. Natural gas—also known as methane—has been championed as a "bridge fuel," one that will help the United States transition off foreign gasoline supplies and onto self-reliance and "cleaner-burning" fuel (relative to coal and gasoline). The heretofore entrapped natural gas fields are scattered across the U.S. While the Barnett Shale in Texas is the most developed, other shales (including the Marcellus) are developing rapidly. At least twenty shale basins have been identified in the country (Andrews, Folger, and Humphries 2009) and many others have been found in other areas of the world. Hence the importance of understanding how this national commodity affects local communities.

Energy Independence

Though in the early years of oil and gas history oil development was dominated by the Texas oil fields ("the Black Giant"—see Margonelli 2007, 103), in the 1930s reserves began to run low. To supplement the supply, the United States turned to the rich oil fields of the Middle East. This move kept cheap oil flowing into the American market, and also bolstered the U.S. presence in the region. With post-World War II conflict with the Soviet Union looming, the United States' connections to the Middle East were strategic both politically and militarily. Import taxes were lowered to encourage low price points and, to the dismay of American oil operators, it actually became cheaper to import oil than to extract oil at home.

Importantly, the use of Middle Eastern oil also shifted the environmental risks associated with the oil and gas industry to lesser developed nations, and moved the environmental consequences out of the U.S. consumer's gaze.

Margonelli (2007, 103) writes that in the years after World War II companies in the Middle East figured out how to use America's increasing dependence on their oil supplies to their political advantage. "Arab oil producers began talking about how to step out of the role of willing and seemingly weak suppliers of oil," she writes, "in order to influence U.S. policy towards Israel."

In 1973, Arab oil producers used this power to their advantage. In retaliation for the United States' support of Israel during the Yom Kippur War, they embargoed oil for the United States and Great Britain.

Gasoline had been a luxury that Americans embraced wholeheartedly, with large, gas-guzzling vehicles, interstate highways, and sprawling suburbs. Car culture reigned and Americans spent hours each week in their cars. With the embargo, prices went up and lines formed at the gas stations. "The gas lines incubated a national loss of identity with geopolitical implications," Margonelli (2007, 103) writes. "The whole definition of being American was that we drove our own cars anywhere we wanted. Public transit and waiting in line was something communists did. In gas lines people turned their anger on each other, and the multinational oil companies, and on an imaginary villain named the 'oil sheikh,' who was usually characterized with an oil can in one hand and a wad of cash in the other, grinning maniacally."

Ripples of the 1973 oil crisis are still felt, and many Americans still resent that the U.S. doesn't control the supply. That crisis, which holds a position in the American collective consciousness, inspires many of the calls for American energy independence.

As has already been noted, one of the arguments in favor of embracing natural gas drilling on U.S. soil is that it could lessen dependence on foreign oil. There are problems with this argument, though. "This argument reflects a myopic calculation of America's national security interests," Klare (2012, 15) writes. "Not only will increased reliance on domestic fossil fuels perpetuate our vulnerability to disorder in the Middle East (given the global nature of the oil market and resulting oil-price dynamics); it will also expose us to a host of other perils, ranging from drinking-water contamination to accelerated climate change." In addition, in an ironic twist, foreign investors have moved to take ownership of American-based gas operations. Charman (2010, 80) writes:

In early 2010, Chesapeake formed a $2.25 billion joint venture with the French energy giant Total that gives Total a twenty-five percent stake in Chesapeake's assets in the Barnett Shale in Texas. India's largest company, Reliance, bought a forty-five percent stake in Pioneer Natural Resources' gas leases in the Eagle Ford Shale in southern Texas after purchasing a forty percent state in Atlas Energy's Marcellus Shale holdings. Oil giants Royal Dutch Shell, ExxonMobil, and ConocoPhillips are also making significant investments in unconventional natural gas in the U.S. and elsewhere, as are Chinese companies.

So much for energy independence. "In our globally connected world," Goodell (2007, xix) writes, "'energy independence' is more of a political slogan than a practical reality."

One of the activists I interviewed spoke at length about the argument for domestic gas drilling as a means of reducing dependence on foreign oil. "This keeps coming up over and over and over," he said. "Every time you talk to one of these dumbasses. 'Well, we need more American fuel.' It's like, all right, look dumbass, gas is not oil. They're not interchangeable at this moment. You know, the post office can run some vehicles on natural gas, but the rest of us don't. It's a blip. There's a glut of natural gas. We have tons of it . . . . I mean, *none* of it comes from terrorist countries. They don't fundamentally understand the difference between oil and gas. They both come out of the ground. That's all they know."

This activist highlights the problems with the foreign-oil-dependence argument. While many power plants have been converting from coal to natural gas (note that the coal—U.S. coal—is primarily domestic already), most vehicles are gasoline powered; extracting more natural gas does not change this fact. Until automobiles are powered by something other than gasoline, the dependence on oil as a fuel source remains.

To promote natural gas development, the 2005 Energy Policy Act granted the natural gas industry $13.5 billion in subsidies (Charman 2010). The companies receive significant tax breaks, paying 0.3 percent on profits rather than the typical 35 percent corporate tax rate (ibid., 79). Gas companies receive these subsidies whether or not their wells produce anything, and that encourages further exploration. Gas companies are also allowed to deduct between 70 percent and 100 percent of the cost of their equipment and supplies. Meanwhile, municipalities receive tax revenues or royalties only when gas production reaches a certain level (ibid., 79). Thus much of the actual cost of gas production is shifted from the gas companies to the tax-paying public.

Support for natural gas development has continued through the Obama administration. "Over the last three years," President Obama said in his 2012 State of the Union speech (cited in Klare 2012, 15), "we've opened millions of new acres for oil and gas exploration."

"When we talk about energy," Goodell writes (2007, xxv), "what we are really talking about is how we live and what we value. Are we willing to put the earth's climate at risk to save ten bucks on our utility bills? To what degree do we want energy corporations to control our access to power? Is it more important to protect yesterday's jobs or to create a new industry for tomorrow? What degree of sacrifice are we willing to make in our lifestyles to ensure the well-being of our children and our grandchildren?" Such questions allude to the complexity of this issue. Americans are not accustomed to interruptions in their power.

Aside from occasional storms that take down power lines, power in this country is reliable, plentiful, and generally affordable. We flip a switch and a light comes on—most people don't think twice about it. "Because we don't see any soot raining down from the sky," Goodell writes (2007, 112), "most of us still think of electricity as a clean, modern, and inexhaustible resource. And power companies are still doing their best to promote consumption, even if they temper it occasionally by paying lip service to conservation and efficiency. After all, they are in the business of selling electricity—and the more you use, the bigger they grow.

2 A Brief Overview of Natural Gas Drilling in Texas

Until recently, oil and gas drilling were confined to rural areas of Texas.

Culturally, urban Texas is very different from rural Texas. Most of the population of the state (with the exception of Houston and El Paso) straddles interstate highway 35. In the so-called I-35 corridor (which includes Dallas, Fort Worth, Waco, Austin, San Antonio, and hundreds of suburban and exurban communities), anyone who throws around cowboy metaphors is likely to inspire eye rolling and sotto voce comments about being an out-of-towner. This is a region of large cities, home to millions of people.

At the northern end of the I-35 corridor lies the Barnett Shale. The Shale encompasses 5,000 square miles, stretching west and south of the Dallas–Fort Worth area into 23 Texas counties. Most of the gas drilling in the Shale takes place in Denton County and Tarrant County. According to the 2010 census, nearly 2.5 million people live in these two counties alone. Urban drilling for natural gas in this region offers a "natural lab"—a case study with which to explore representations of community-level health threats.

In 1981, Mitchell Energy drilled the first natural gas well in the Barnett Shale (a well that is still producing gas today). With developments in hydrofracturing and horizontal drilling, natural gas development began in earnest in the Barnett Shale in the late 1990s. By 2005 the Shale was producing 10 percent of the nation's natural gas. As of January 2012, there were 16,530 natural gas wells in the Barnett Shale, and an additional 2,457 locations had received permits to begin drilling. There were also 195 commercial disposal wells, which hold water that has been used in hydraulic fracturing (Texas Railroad Commission 2013).

Shale is organic-rich sedimentary rock. It is highly permeable, and has the potential to hold large quantities of natural gas. Due to the physical structure of shale, it is not easy to get the gas out of the ground. Natural gas is trapped inside the rock, and has been likened to "bubbles in fossilized soda" (Schmidt 2011, 348). To extract the gas, a bore is drilled deep into the earth vertically. In most cases, the drill then takes a horizontal turn and may continue outward for up to a mile. Hydraulic fracturing is then used to break up the rock and allow gas to flow up the pipe to the surface.

Shale gas is also called "unconventional gas," because methods of obtaining shale gas have been less explored until recent years. Historically, natural gas was obtained by what is now known as "conventional" means. Conventional gas is a by-product of oil production. The gas may either be a cap at the top of the oil well or may be found below the "oil window," which is located at a depth of between 7,500 and 15,000 feet. At depths greater than 15,000 feet, oil molecules become unstable and split apart into gas. During oil production, natural gas may also be injected into an oil well to build an artificial gas cap. The pressure created by the gas cap allows for greater oil recovery while preserving the gas for future extraction (Deffeyes 2005).

Five different types of unconventional gas exist. Swamp gas is formed when bacteria convert organic matter into methane. Swamp gas fields are small, but may be profitable for smaller companies and may serve as a source of fuel in underdeveloped regions of the world. Coal-bed gas is another unconventional source of natural gas, as are basin-center gas (associated with tight sand rock) and gas hydrates (a crystalline frozen gas-water mix). Finally, and relevant to this discussion, is fractured shale gas (Deffeyes 2005, 53–55).

The gas industry has known about unconventional sources of gas for more than a hundred years; however, extracting that gas was not technologically feasible for the industry until recently. According to Goodell (2012), "geologists had long known there was a lot more energy buried deep underground—they called these subterranean rock layers 'the kitchen' because it was where the gas and oil were actually made, before they bubbled up and gathered in reserves. But nobody knew how to extract these deep reserves—at least, not in a way that made economic sense."

However, the oil and gas industry has learned how to tap those reserves in recent years. Two technological developments opened shale gas reserves: horizontal drilling and advances in hydraulic fracturing. (Although technological advances have expanded the ability to tap new stores, the basic processes involved in extracting oil and gas today would not be foreign to the roughnecks of the early oil boom.)

Shale gas is plentiful in the United States, and there are "plays" (as the industry calls them) in many states (Wilber 2012). Texas has the longest history of active natural gas extraction, and community responses to natural gas development in Texas can serve as case studies for other communities undergoing the process.

In popular discourse, there seems to be misperception that gas fields in Texas are removed from the population centers. As will be shown in this book, communities are coexisting (although not always well) with the activities, and millions of Texans are directly affected by natural gas activities.

What Happens at a Natural Gas Site

To understand how drilling and other activities involved in the extraction of natural gas affect urban residents, it is important to understand what happens during those activities. Various zones are established within cities to separate industry from homes to the extent possible because of the disruptive effects as well as because of potential harm to residents. Extracting and transporting natural gas are industrial activities that have been placed in pre-existing residential zones rather than in industrial zones.

Natural gas extraction takes place in three stages (McKenzie et al. 2012). In the first stage, the well is drilled and then "completed" with concrete casings. Once that process is finished, hydraulic fracturing is done to release the natural gas. In the third stage, "flowback" (a water-based solution that flows back to the surface during and after the completion of hydraulic fracturing) and natural gas rise to the surface. The gas portion contains not only methane but also a host of other gases, chemicals, and liquids, many of which are toxic and must be removed before the gas can be used.

The drill rig is probably the most visible component of the extraction process. Drills range from 90 to 120 feet tall, depending on the type of cut that is used. The rigs themselves look the same for both oil and gas, and they use similar techniques. Gas wells do not have pump jacks, as oil wells do. Rather, compression engines are used to pump out the gas. These engines run continuously, can be quite noisy, and are often diesel powered, with associated exhaust emissions.

Margonelli (2007, 68) describes her first encounter with a natural gas drilling rig this way:

At the end of the road stands the derrick. I enter the square garrison of trailers around its base, park, and open my car door to a stunning wall of 100-degree heat and throbbing noise—*cachunk cachunk*. By the time I stand up this sound has segued into pounding vibrations beyond my hearing. I feel seasick.

McGraw (2011, 97) writes about "just how disruptive—how explosively, bone-jarringly disruptive—natural gas drilling is":

The wild roar of the diesel generators was deafening, to be sure, but it was nothing compared to the sound of the drill, the screech of iron on iron, of carbide on stone, a bone-rattling thunder that shook the distant trees and churned the dull gray mud that covered my boots to the ankles.

Drilling a well can take two weeks or more. In the first day of drilling, the surface casing is set into place. This is a steel pipe that is fed down the hole and then sealed in place with cement. Its purpose is to prevent contamination of groundwater, so it is important this step be performed properly.

Developments in drilling technology now allow for horizontal drilling. Initially, a well is drilled vertically down into the shale bed. The drill then turns and extends through the rock layer horizontally. This allows for much greater release of gas using only one well pad. A pad can be placed at the edge of a neighborhood, and then the well can be drilled horizontally underneath homes.

Fracking

After completion of the drilling, hydraulic fracturing ("fracking") is used to crack open the rock with hundreds of micro-fractures and release the natural gas. Gas will not flow out of the shale without this step. Though it is just one stage in the extraction process, fracking has captured the popular imagination and tends to be the focal point in discussions about natural gas development. Between 3 million and 7 million gallons of "frack water" are pumped down the pipe at a pressure of more than 9,000 pounds per square inch (McGraw 2011). This explosive pressure creates cracks in the rock layer up to 3,000 feet in every direction around the bore (Andrews, Folger, and Humphries 2009). Each well is fracked several times over the course of its lifetime. This adds up to a tremendous use of fresh water.

"Frack water" consists mainly of fresh water, and includes a propping agent or proppant (synthetic sand used to keep the fractures open) and a number of chemicals. The chemicals added to the fracturing fluid include "friction reducers, surfactants, gelling agents, scale inhibitors, acids, corrosion inhibitors, antibacterial agents, and clay stabilizers" (Jackson et al. 2012, 2). The chemicals in the "frack fluid" vary with the mineral composition of the rock formation. Frack fluid is toxic to human health.

Until quite recently, in Texas all components of fracking fluid were considered proprietary, and therefore companies were not bound by requirements to disclose the ingredients. In June of 2011, the Texas Legislature mandated disclosure of components of fracking fluid. Nonetheless, there are still workarounds to this ruling to protect proprietary interests. Owing to the secrecy surrounding fracking fluid's exact formation, it is perhaps not surprising that concerns were raised about safety and public health. What was being injected into the ground? How would it affect the aquifers, the soil, and human health? These were (and still are) unanswered questions.

Flowback

Used frack water is also called "flowback"—it is literally the water that flows back out of the well, pushed out by the freed natural gas. Not all of the frack water returns to the surface. That which does return to the surface contains not only the original chemicals but also compounds pulled up from beneath the ground, including brine, heavy metals, and naturally occurring radioactive materials. Flowback is classified as hazardous waste and must be disposed of properly.

According to Andrews, Folger, and Humphries (2009, 1), "the saline 'flowback' water pumped back to the surface after the fracturing process poses a significant environmental management challenge." While there are some companies trying to recycle and reuse at least some of the flowback, that water is contaminated, and it cannot be reintroduced into the hydrological cycle. In Texas, most of it is put back into the ground in deep injection wells. Many community members argue that this practice has caused notable increase in both the numbers and magnitude of earthquakes in the region. (This is not an area with active fault lines.) At present the U.S. Environmental Protection Agency doesn't regulate fracking, and the process is exempt from the Safe Water Drinking Act, which normally regulates deep injection of any waste water in order to protect underground aquifers.

Along with the fracking fluid, a number of compounds are drawn to the surface during flowback, including natural salts, toxins, and naturally occurring radioactive materials. These must be disposed of in a manner that will not contaminate the air or the water or further contribute to global climate change.

According to Jackson et al. (2012, 3), the amount of flowback can range from 15 percent to 80 percent of the amount of fracturing fluid, and "during the first month of drilling and production alone, a single well can produce a million or more gallons of wastewater that can contain pollutants in concentrations far exceeding those considered safe for drinking water and for release into the environment. These pollutants sometimes include formaldehyde, boric acid, methanol, hydrochloric acid, and isopropanol, which can damage the brain, eyes, skin, and nervous system on direct contact. Another potential type of contamination comes from naturally occurring salts, metals, and radioactive chemicals found deep underground."

What began as millions of gallons of fresh water is now millions of gallons of hazardous waste.

In addition, "produced water" flows from a well throughout its lifetime. When the gas comes to the surface, it is mixed with other compounds, such as water, liquid hydrocarbons (including benzene, toluene, ethylbenzene, and xylene), and hydrogen sulfide (Colborn et al. 2011). These compounds must be distilled from the gas in condensate tanks. Produced water also must be disposed of. In some cases, it is put in open-air pits and left to evaporate. According to Andrews, Folger, and Humphries (2009), "the well service company may temporarily retain the flowback and brine in open-air, lined retention ponds before reusing it (if possible), or disposing it." In Texas, the liquid must be collected into a tanker truck and transported to an injection well, where it is forced back underground.

Flaring

Once a well has been drilled and fracked and the flowback has been captured, the gas begins to flow. The well is then "flared" to remove excess gas and get rid of contaminants in "a huge, controlled open-air flame" (Deffeyes

2005, 56). One activist told me about the flaring of a well on a golf course in the center of a neighborhood:

They build a big pit and they put something in there that looks like a gigantic bar-beque grill distributor and they flame it all out there under the ground. So at one point on that golf course there was a pit ten feet deep that had flames that were coming four or five feet out of the ground for weeks as they were flaring that thing. They didn't want to. [But they] felt it was a safer alternative to the traditional flaring, which is just a big pipe stuck up in the air.

Some companies forgo flaring in favor of "green completion." This process captures the excess gas rather than venting it or flaring it off. Some cities' oil and gas ordinances now require green completions for all wells.

The Pad Site

The pad site—the entire site of the operation—takes up about half a city block, with staging areas often filled with diesel trucks, and either an open pit (which looks like a large, rectangular holding pond lined with plastic) or a closed tank to store used frack water. One pad may have multiple wells on the site.

Estimates vary on the amount of truck traffic to each site. According to a 2005 Denton County report, each drilling site requires 364 round trips just to bring fracking fluid to the site. The legal weight limit of the trucks used for this is 80,000 pounds each, which creates a tremendous impact on roads and bridges that typically were not designed with this level of activity in mind.

After drilling, a "Christmas tree," processing devices, and storage tanks are put into place. Some wells, particularly older ones, are outfitted with diesel or electric compression engines to help to move the gas along the pipelines.

Pipelines

The pads are connected with a network of distribution pipes. Natural gas is delivered to power plants and other destinations across the country by means of a large pipeline infrastructure. More than 300,000 miles of pipeline have already been built in the United States (Rahm 2011). Along the routes, compressor (or pumping) stations are required to keep the gas moving. The pipelines are under tremendous pressure and are susceptible to explosion. Such explosions have already been documented. Nonetheless, there are pipelines in close proximity to schoolyards and residential neighborhoods. Malfunctions in pipelines can be catastrophic for the receiving plants (Goodell 2007, 74) as well as for the residents living nearby.

One activist pointed out a green belt on the map of her city. "This is the big pipeline that goes through town," she explained. "Where we put our jogging trails on top of. People want to live next to it because we have all the beautiful jogging trails." She sighed. She has seen enough reports of pipeline disasters on the Internet to believe that none of this is a good idea.

The pipeline infrastructure also limits future development by laying claim to large swaths of land. Structures cannot be built on top of the pipelines.

Raising Alarm

In many areas of the Barnett Shale, towns and neighborhoods were inhabited before natural gas development began. In fact, the Dallas–Fort Worth metroplex has been one of the fastest growing areas in the nation. Many people, particularly among the middle class, purchased homes there unaware that they would eventually find themselves living next to industrial activities.

Home ownership has long been one of the main components of the so-called American Dream. And despite the recent recession, construction of new homes is rampant in the Dallas–Fort Worth metroplex. Houses are quite affordable relative to other parts of the country; nice new homes ranging from 1,500 to 3,000 square feet are priced between $100,000 and $300,000. One's home is generally thought of as a place of safety and security. Environmentally polluting industry threatens that sense of well-being.

One activist explained to me how she became concerned about the possible health implications of natural gas drilling:

There's this blogger I read. She lives just a few miles from me. She started seeing weird stuff in her yard, basically what looked like bubbling frack fluid in her yard. Well, come to find out, she has well water, and her well water is contaminated. They've tested her water and it's contaminated. You know on *Gasland*, which is an HBO movie, where they light the water on fire?

I nodded. (It's a dramatic scene, watching water pouring from a tap and shooting off flames. It happens when a water well is contaminated with methane.) The activist continued:

OK, so she's like 'Oh, well, that's amazing, let me see if my water catches on fire.' She goes to light her water, and she videotaped it. This was my seminal moment. She videotapes lighting her water. It didn't light, but after she got done holding the flame to her water, like in a glass container, she put her hand in the water and went like this [here she swished her hand around], and it looked like Saran Wrap. Plastic hanging off her hand, literally looked like Saran Wrap in her water. I was like 'That's petrochemicals!' I mean, if there's plastic, if you can make plastic with flame, you have petrochemicals in your water. I looked at the distance between her house and mine, and I want to say it was like a mile and a half. That really worried me. When I tell my friends, they think I'm crazy to be worried because we're on public water, we're not on wells, and this woman lives in the next town, not ours. But in my view, the last time I checked, the aquifer is not smart enough to know the city limits, right? If her water is contaminated, the water under my house could be contaminated. Now I'm not drinking it, but there's naturally fed spring ponds near here. Sometimes in the spring when there's a lot of rain, the groundwater comes up into people's yards. Who wants contaminated water under their feet?"

"And their kids are running around in the back yard?" I asked.

"Exactly," she replied

Encroachment of natural gas operations into the population centers of North Texas has raised alarm. Residents question how their proximity will affect public health and safety as well as the natural environment. Though natural gas development was initially supported by many national environmental organizations for its potential to be both a bridge fuel and a cleaner alternative to gasoline and coal, many environmentalists now oppose its extraction because of health and other concerns. Also, methane itself is a powerful greenhouse gas. According to Bruce Hamilton, executive director of the Sierra Club (as quoted on page 24 of Tuhus 2011), natural gas

is a fossil fuel, it's dirty, its leading to major contamination of the planet, both from a global warming standpoint and an ecosystem standpoint. At one point when people thought natural gas was twice as clean as coal from a greenhouse gas emission standpoint, many environmental groups suggested natural gas was a good alternative and what we used to call a "transition" or "bridge" fuel. But that basic assumption . . . was based on faulty, outdated information.

The Natural Resources Defense Council also switched from supporting development of natural gas (Tuhus 2011).

Although there are clear benefits to the use of natural gas as an energy source, there are also many drawbacks. As in many environmental justice narratives, there is a need to balance profit with safety, and to ensure that the public is protected from harm.

Both George W. Bush and Barack Obama may have likened our consumption of oil to an addiction, but Jeff Goodell (2007, xiii–xiv) carries the metaphor further when discussing natural gas:

If coal was our industrial smack, natural gas was our methadone: It was clean, easy to transport, and nearly as cheap as coal. Virtually every power plant built in America between 1975 and 2002 was gas-fired. Almost everybody in the energy world presumed that the natural gas era would soon give way to even cleaner sources of power generation—wind, solar, biofuels, hydrogen, perhaps someday solar panels on the moon . . . . But like many revolutions, this one hasn't progressed quite as planned.

The natural gas industry has been credited for job creation and for booms in the Texas economy, and has been cited as one of the main reasons that Texas has suffered less from the recent national recession than other states (EnergyFromShale 2013). One study found that 312,000 Texans work in the oil and gas industry and that that industry accounts for 14.9 percent ($159.3 billion) of Texas' gross state product (State Impact 2013).

Not everyone is happy with the arrival of gas operations, however. Grassroots organizations have emerged out of the cities and towns of the Barnett Shale. Grassroots organizers have focused on two areas of concern: property rights and perceived threats to public health. Early in the process, activists were concerned primarily with air pollution. Since then, however, they have focused more and more on water use and water pollution. Additionally, fears of cancer permeate the narrative—fears that are heightened by data that suggest increasing cancer incidence in Barnett Shale communities.

3   Activists' Concerns about Health

Ahmed is afraid of storms. He's afraid of what happens at a natural gas pad site when a storm knocks out the power. "I was literally gassed in my own home in the middle of the night," he tells me. He continues:

It sounds very sensationalized. We lost power because of a wicked storm that blew through. We heard an explosion that was like a transformer that must have blown. It threw the compressor station offline. Pressure built up in the system here. I had opened the windows after the storm passed and a cool front had blown in. I like the fresh air. And then we heard this. Venting like this: ZHHHZHHHZHHH. Really loud. It jolted us up. I heard this noise and I started to shake. I was terrified. I thought, oh my gosh, what is happening? I knew it was off the [gas] site because I could hear what direction it was coming from. So then I called 911. My house filled with gas or something. I don't even know what it was, but it stunk. It smelled dirty. It smelled like . . . like the inside of a bicycle tube tire. Maybe kind of what that would smell like. It was very strong and it rushed into my house because the winds were whipping from all directions that night.

Ahmed's concerns were supported by a report from the Texas Commission on Environmental Quality (TCEQ) that the gas well near his home had vented as a result of increases in pressure and by email messages from the company that owned the well. Both the TCEQ and the company reported the event as small, with low amounts of gas released. But Ahmed believes that the release was much bigger than the records from that night indicate:

They've got to burp that stuff out or it will explode. It covered the neighborhood like a heavy, it had a heavy feel, and I'm feeling like a crazy person because everyone is telling me nothing is lighter than air and it just dissipates and it's odorless. Well, what was this? This was something else. I still, to this day, do not know what we were exposed to. And I'm looking at my eleven-year-old daughter lying in bed, innocently sleeping, and I'm thinking "Oh my gosh, she's getting gassed in her sleep.

She's getting a chemical exposure." So we're quickly shutting the windows, but it was too late. All the gunk was already in there and you couldn't go outside.

General Concerns about Chemicals and Pollution

When fossil fuels are used in the generation of electricity, environmental pollution follows. Health effects from pollution tend to be noticed in animals first. Mutations. Die-offs (sometimes massive). Birth defects. Tumors. Cancers. Infertility. And then people begin to ask "If animals are being impacted by toxic pollutants, how are the pollutants affecting our health?"

"That environmental stuff in the air is stressing the trees," one activist told me. We walked around her neighborhood. She wanted to show me evidence of pollution from the natural gas wells there. "That's what I think." She points toward the gas pad on her street. "Because if you look to the houses that back up to the well site . . . a lot of the tops of the trees are dying."

She is right. The trees she points to are brown, in a neighborhood of green. "If the trees are dying," she asks, "what's happening to me?"

A stew of chemicals is involved in the process of extracting gas. Many chemicals are used to access and release the gas. Many more are brought up out of the ground. This toxic soup has alarmed many people who live near wells. What, if any, impact does exposure to these chemicals have on human health? What is the impact on the environment?

Possible health effects related to natural gas drilling came to the fore in the Barnett Shale discourse and gained national media attention via outcries from a small town called Dish. The town had a population of 262 in 2012, but it is in close proximity to larger cities. It is about 30 miles north of Fort Worth. Formerly known as Clark, the town changed its name in 2005 in a deal with the satellite TV service Dish. For making the change, the residents all received ten years of free Dish TV. Unfortunately, not all of their dealings with corporations have been so successful.

Just across the delineation line of the city limits, several large compression stations were constructed—stations that pump and process natural gas through the pipelines (see *Town of Dish v. Atmos Energy Corp et al.* 2011). The site of those stations is enormous and loud. Foliage between the site and the town turned brown and died. Cows and horses exhibited neurological symptoms and aborted fetuses. Some of the residents also began to have neurological symptoms (Wilson et al. 2011). At the behest of the residents, the mayor used town funds to pay for a consulting firm to test the air quality around the compression station. The consulting firm found high levels of hydrocarbons emanating from the compression engine exhaust and from the exhaust of the diesel vehicles that frequented the site. Heavy metals were identified—not unexpectedly, in view of the large volume of industrial equipment at the site. The consulting firm also found excessively high levels of benzene and other toxic chemicals in the air in Dish—levels exceeding health and safety limits specified by state regulators. Immediately after the consulting firm released its report, its methodology was criticized by the industry and its findings were disputed. Nevertheless, those findings raised significant alarm.

In response, the Texas Department of State Health Services (DSHS) Toxicology Unit conducted a human health study in Dish to research the impact of the chemical exposures (Bradford et al. 2010). Investigators collected blood and urine from a sample of adult residents and sampled tap water from homes. Their report noted, but did not specify the amounts of, odor and noise associated with the industrial activity. The investigators used themselves as a control group, sampling their own blood and urine before leaving Austin and then again after spending time in Dish. The levels of contaminants found were compared against data from the National Health and Nutrition Examination Survey to determine if the residents of Dish had higher levels of the chemicals in their bodies than people in the general population.

Volatile organic compounds—chemicals known to cause cancer—were found in some of the blood samples. But were they attributable to exposure to the natural gas activities, or to other sources? Most of the people with positive findings were cigarette smokers, and their cigarettes could have been the source of the chemicals. Other possible sources were identified in the DSHS report as well. The report stated that the results were not significantly different from results in the general population. The report recommended continued observation and referral of people with symptoms to their health care providers. Like the report from the environmental consultant's air study, the findings of the DSHS's study were questioned, this time by environmental activists. The activists argued that the state's methodology and its statistical analysis were flawed.

In the state's defense, some of the methodological problems are acknowl-
edged in the department's report (DSHS 2010):

This investigation did have limitations. First, [volatile organic compounds] only stay
in the body for a short time (several hours); therefore these measurements only reflect ongoing or recent exposures. Second, this was a one time sampling event; thus
it could not consider variations in factors such as season, temperature, wind conditions, and natural gas operations. Third, we could not identify with any degree of
certainty a source for all of the exposures. Fourth, the urinary metabolite AMCA is
not completely specific and can form through other metabolic pathways. Lastly,
it was not possible to determine potential health risks based on the levels found in
the blood.

The DSHS report concluded, therefore, that "the information obtained
from this investigation did not indicate that community-wide exposures
from gas wells or compressor stations were occurring in the sample population." "This conclusion," the report continued, "is based on the pattern of
VOC values found in the samples. Other sources of exposure such as cigarette smoking, the presence of disinfectant by-products in [the town] drinking water and consumer or occupational/hobby related products could
explain many of the findings."

The research of the consulting company and the state agency demonstrates the difficulty involved in proving that a particular exposure caused
a particular illness. "It is a complex dance," Nichols writes (2008, 8),
"between an individual and his or her environment that leads to disease."
This complex dance complicates the ability to assign blame.

Drilling for natural gas, particularly in urban areas, has not been accompanied by studies that demonstrate its safety (Finkle and Law 2011). "We
really don't know what the health effects are of drilling in an urban environment," one city official told me.

Perhaps the most comprehensive study to date on the potential health
effects of natural gas drilling is a review of the literature conducted by the
Colorado School of Public Health (Witter et al. 2008). The authors reviewed
831 peer-reviewed scientific articles, all published between 2003 and 2008.
Contaminants of concern included volatile organic compounds (VOCs),
diesel exhaust, nitrogen and sulfuric oxides (NO_x, SO_x), ozone, particulate
matter, polycyclic aromatic hydrocarbons (PAHs), heavy metals, hydrogen
sulfide, and other hazardous chemicals within the fracking fluids. All of
these compounds have been identified at natural gas operations in the

Barnett Shale. Local environmental investigative companies as well the Texas Commission on Environmental Quality have repeatedly documented the presence of VOCs and other toxic chemicals at natural gas sites.

Another group of researchers (Colborn et al. 2011) used the Material Safety Data Sheets for known chemicals used in natural gas operations to create so-called health effects profiles. Although industry representatives often argue that the amounts of the chemicals in fracking fluid are too low to cause harm to human health, the researchers argue that toxicity pathways are not well understood and therefore this is not a valid argument. Hundreds of toxic chemicals are associated with gas operations, and many of them may cause numerous types of health effects. In addition, the health effects of many of the chemicals are unknown, and there are woefully few data on interaction effects. Colborn et al. and others write that simply not enough actions are being taken by regulatory and public health agencies to protect health and safety.

Additional research into the known components of fracking fluids reveals that they contain many compounds that are known to be toxic to human health and many known and suspected carcinogens. One study found chemicals within fracking fluids that cause a significant number of health effects, including cancer; reproductive disruptions; skin, eye, and respiratory symptoms; impairments of the brain and the central nervous system; and gastrointestinal and liver disease (Finkle and Law 2011). Also found were some known endocrine disruptors, the effects of which can manifest years or even decades after exposure, not only in the people exposed but also in their offspring (Langston 2010).

Researchers in Colorado found that people living within half a mile of a natural gas well are significantly more likely to develop critical health effects, including cancer, than people living more than half a mile from the site (McKenzie et al. 2012). This research is particularly interesting because it was conducted in a rural area that has very low vehicular pollution and in which the only other industry is agriculture. Thus the researchers could clearly point to gas development as problematic for human health. In contrast, residents in the Barnett Shale are exposed to multiple sources of pollution, with an even higher burden of chemical exposure.

Of course, methane is highly explosive. In 1944, liquid natural gas leaked into the sewer system in Cleveland and exploded, killing 128 people. In 1973, a natural gas-related explosion on Staten Island killed 37 workers. In

2004, an explosion in Algeria killed between 20 and 30 people (Deffeyes 2005, 78). On smaller scales, pipeline explosions are not infrequent, nor are home explosions. Explosion threats are not hypothetical; explosions have occurred in the Barnett Shale and in other natural gas fields.

According to representatives of the industry, however, reports of health threats are highly exaggerated. They insist their practices are safe. But in the discourse of the local communities, the emerging representation is that urban natural gas drilling presents a serious threat to public health.

Toxic Burden

Edelstein (2004, 9) writes that "environmental hazards (1) are ubiquitous and (2) are often invisible in the landscape. Unless we are truly looking for them."

One activist showed me data that she had collected from an air monitor in the Barnett Shale. She had charted daily levels of benzene, and had identified a particularly high spike in the readings. She told me this about her experience of sharing the data with a state regulator:

He just went right to my Excel spreadsheet and said "Oh yeah, we were concerned about that when it happened. Boy, that was a big outlier, that was the worst in the metroplex!" I was stunned. That's when I went back and I pulled down all the readings from [other monitors in the Shale], and I was like, "Holy crap!" Because . . . no, after how hard I fight here, I always believe that we've got it better than everybody else. And I believed that—I still believe that, actually, because I've been to people's homes that are right next to [air quality] collection points like we have. You can't go there without getting ill. You can't go there without your eyes burning, your lips burning.

Statistically speaking, *outliers* are singular values so far outside the expected range that one generally discards them during analysis. That is unfortunate, because, as in this case, outliers can also be indicators of serious problems.

On multiple occasions, at multiple sites across the Shale, the Texas Commission on Environmental Quality has documented benzene and other toxins at levels higher than the agency's specified long-term health effects levels. Volatile organic compounds are found at natural gas pads and are released into the air during transportation activities. Little research has been conducted on low-dose, long-term exposure to these chemicals. They are known to be neurotoxins, to affect both the central nervous system and the peripheral nervous system, and to contribute to cognitive and behavioral changes. They are also toxic to the liver and the reproductive system. They are toxic to fetuses, and can cause miscarriages and low birth weight. They contribute to cancers, leukemia in particular. Benzene, one of the VOCs, is a known carcinogen. Trichloroethylene and dichloromethane, also found associated with gas extraction, are classified as probable human carcinogens.

The International Agency for Research on Cancer (IARC) maintains a classification of the carcinogenicity of certain chemicals. Group 1 agents are those that are conclusively known to be carcinogenic to humans. Benzene and shale oils are group 1 agents. Group 2A agents are probably carcinogenic to humans, and group 2B agents are possibly cancer causing. Diesel exhaust is classified as a 2A agent, and toluene (also found associated with natural gas sites) is classified as 2B. Group 3 agents are those for which there isn't enough information to determine whether or not they cause cancer, and group 4 agents are thought not likely to be carcinogenic to humans.

In order for a substance to be listed by the IARC as even a possible carcinogen, a significant amount of scientific research has to have been performed and debated. Controversies concerning some toxins have gone unresolved for decades. Standards of proof have become increasingly stronger in recent years. "In the past," Davis writes (2002, 142), "if a study exposure caused cancer in lab animals, it was regarded as a threat to humans. No more." Rather, data from research studies demonstrating clear cause and effects in humans became the "gold standard" for labeling a compound as a carcinogen. Such data are difficult to obtain. Ethically, one cannot expose a group of humans to a chemical and watch to see what happens. Instead, most human studies involve large-dose exposure accidents and exposures to employees in industrial settings. One must ask whose interests are involved by setting such a high standard of proof. In the meantime, those chemicals are still used. While the safety of a particular compound is in dispute, however, debating whether or not it causes harm does not render it harmless.

Diesel exhaust from engines at natural gas sites and from the heavy trucks frequenting the sites presents a variety of human health hazards, including releases of particulate matter, heavy metals, and other organic compounds, and is associated with cardiovascular disease, respiratory illness, allergies, genetic changes in chromosomes and DNA, and increases in childhood illnesses.

Nitrogen oxides (NO_x), sulfur oxides (SO_x), ozone, and particulate matter are released at several points in natural gas production. These compounds are associated with respiratory disease, childhood asthma, cardiovascular disease, genetic changes in chromosomes and DNA, harm to fetal and neonatal health, and increased mortality.

Particulate matter (10 microns or less) is associated with a number of health effects, and is especially hazardous to children and the elderly. Particulate matter is carried deep into the lungs upon inhalation. The particles are so small that they can cross the blood barrier and be deposited anywhere in the body. They are sticky, and can carry along other toxic pollutants into the body. For every increase of 10 micrograms per cubic meter in the amount of particulate matter inhaled, the death rate in the exposed population increases by 0.05 percent (Goodell 2007, 128–129). Though that increase seems small, when multiplied over millions of people it is significant—and there are millions of people living in the Barnett Shale. Deaths from pneumonia, lung disease, and heart attacks increase in a population along with increases in particulate matter (ibid., 129). Even smaller particulate matter has been demonstrated to affect health. Recent research on ultra-fine particulate matter (with particles 0.1 micron in diameter, about the size of an average bacterium) has found that these particles move from the lungs directly into the bloodstream, bypassing the usual filtering activities of the lungs. They may also transverse the blood-brain barrier. According to one estimate cited by Goodell (ibid., 133), "about 14 percent of the ultrafines we breathe pass straight to our brains."

Polycyclic aromatic hydrocarbons (PAHs) are associated with immune dysfunction, reproductive harm, and low birth weight and other fetal problems. Heavy metals, also found associated with gas drilling, can lead to a variety of health problems. Lead, for example, is a known neurotoxin and is associated with increased cancer risks. Arsenic is associated with DNA changes, cancer, renal dysfunction, and reproductive problems.

"Sour" gas (that is, gas with high levels of hydrogen sulfide) is flammable and smells similar to rotten eggs. Hydrogen sulfide (H_2S), which is fatal at high doses and can cause neurological damage at lower doses, is one of the few compounds whose long-term, low-dose effects have been studied. Researchers have found depression, memory loss, and other neuro-psychological effects associated with it. High hospitalization rates from respiratory effects (including asthma, pneumonia, and chronic obstructive pulmonary disorder) have been observed in communities subjected to low-dose, chronic H_2S exposure. Although some H_2S is released into the atmosphere as a result of accidents and equipment failures, the industry catches most of it and converts it into elemental sulfur, which is then used in the manufacturing of fertilizers, pharmaceuticals, plastics, and other products. The remaining H_2S is usually burned in flares or incinerators that results in the conversion of H_2S to sulfur dioxide (SO_2), small quantities of other toxic compounds, such as carbonyl sulfide (COS) and carbon disulfide (CS_2), nitrogen oxides (NO_x), and volatile organic compounds (Boxall, Chan, and McMillan 2005, 250). Humans can smell H_2S at concentrations as low as 0.01 ppm; however, above concentrations of 100 ppm, the sense is deadened and humans can no longer smell the threat. At 1–5 ppm, H_2S can cause nausea and headache. At 50–250 ppm, the olfactory system can suffer paralysis. At 300–500 ppm, death is likely (ibid. 2005, 250). One activist told me: "What we've learned, and this is anecdotal information, but what we've learned talking to people who live close [to gas-extraction activities] is that certain people have almost like an allergy or intolerance to what's going on. And a lot of them think it has to do with the sulfides that are being spit out [of the wells]."

"Everybody's focus is on benzene," another activist told me. She continued:

Last year, some environmentalist guy from Oregon sent me an email, he said "Hey, I want you to go to these links and read them, they [the industry] try to get you to focus on benzene but you need to look at carbon disulfide, you really need to look at it." I've got all the studies that were done related to carbon disulfide. And carbon disulfide is very interesting because it seems to be found in close proximity to compression stations. It may or may not be a direct result of fracking, but it definitely seems to be in concert with compression stations. TCEQ doesn't routinely look for carbon disulfide. Because we raised such a ruckus in [our city] about carbon disulfide, [the city] started surveying for carbon disulfide. And they found short-term ESLs at 69 parts per billion. The short term ESL is 10.

Effects screening levels (ESLs) are used by the TCEQ to determine when pollutants are at levels unsafe for human health. Short-term measurements are based on sampling for an average of one hour; long-term measurements are averaged over a year (TCEQ 2013a). "If predicted airborne levels of a constituent do not exceed the screening level," according to the TCEQ (ibid.), "adverse health or welfare effects are not expected. If predicted ambient levels of constituents in air exceed the screening levels, it does not necessarily indicate a problem but rather triggers a review in more depth." Probably not surprisingly, there is debate about where these levels are set. Levels vary from state to state, and Texas is more liberal in the amounts of chemicals people may be exposed to before concern is raised than other areas of the United States. Some activists worry that the set thresholds fail to account for variations in vulnerable populations, such as very young children, the elderly, and people with severe chronic health conditions.

There are even questions about the safety of methane itself. Methane in drinking water is not regulated, aside from the asphyxiation and explosion hazards. There have been essentially no peer-reviewed scientific studies on the health effects of drinking methane-contaminated water. However, instances of home explosions tied directly to water contamination due to faulty gas-well casings have been scientifically documented (Jackson et al. 2012).

Studying the effects of the environment on health is difficult and involves an intersecting assemblage of factors (Gibbs 2007). The causality between environmental exposures to toxins and illness is seldom straightforward. Multiple variables are involved in illness, and it is often difficult to scientifically ascertain that exposure to a particular toxin caused a specific incidence of illness in a population. There is a significant lack of scientific evidence to point to when exploring causality. We simply do not understand the intricacies of how chemicals affect the human body. Although there are studies that show harmful effects from chemical exposures, the literature is not clear as to the mechanisms of this effect. Available studies are often modeled on animal subjects, since (as I have already noted) it would be unethical to expose a human to certain chemicals just to see what would happen. Compounding the problem is the additional burden of multiple interacting chemicals in the system. Although we may have a good understanding of the physiological effects of benzene (for example) on the body, we do not know the combined effect of benzene and other toxins inside the body. Finally, the exploration of environmentally caused illness is blocked by the powerful financial interests of multibillion-dollar industries. Should definitive linkages between chemical exposure and illness be identified, the impact on corporate interests could be huge.

Researchers typically consider toxins in isolation, yet in reality humans are exposed to multiple toxins from multiple sources at a time. What this all means is unclear, and this lack of clarity contributes to fears expressed in the Shale narrative.

Early in the history of toxicology, researchers sought to identify the levels of exposure to a toxin at which a person would be expected to die. In lab tests in the 1950s, animals that survived exposure to chemicals were presumed to be confirmatory evidence that the chemicals were safe (Davis 2002). Toxicologists worked to develop antidotes to various poisons. One lab test, known as the LD50, measured the amount of time it took for half of the animals in a test group to die from exposure to a particular toxin. Although the LD50 test was used until the 1980s, in the 1950s researchers documented that the age of the animal at the time of exposure was a significant variable (ibid.). Very young animals were more susceptible to the effects of toxins than older, more developed animals. Animal studies also showed that small daily doses of a toxin could cause more damage to the lungs than a shorter-term, higher dose. In addition, low-dose long-term exposure to some toxins caused permanent lung damage.

When considering such studies, researchers hold underlying assumptions that disease processes in animals mimic expected finding in humans. Yet not all scientists accept this view. A human is different from a rat, of course, but how different when it comes to chemicals? Do death rates after toxic exposures in rats accurately reflect the potential for harm in humans? We don't really know. We can't expose a test group of humans to potentially toxic chemicals and record the death rate.

All of the previously mentioned contaminants have been identified in association with gas activities in the Barnett Shale. Concerns have been raised about how these compounds pollute the air and drinking water, and about other damage to the natural environment, such as soil contamination during the disposal of drilling sludge.

Air Pollution

Davis (2002, 268) quotes Sam Wyly, the founder of Green Mountain Energy and a resident of Dallas, as having said the following in a speech: "The stars at night are no longer big and bright. A brown haze, which I used to see on trips to Los Angeles or Taipei, has slowly been creeping across the Dallas sky. The problem has hit home."

"I don't know if you've been to [a certain city]," one activist said to me. "There's a couple of big sites right around them. The neighbors there, that neighborhood complains of a lot of problems. People tell me 'Well, there's so many kids that go to school every day and have bloody noses or sore throats.' And looking at the TCEQ complaints and it's . . . they're complaining about a sulfur smell." (I left the city unnamed in that statement intentionally. Because this is a story I heard so many times, most of the cities with active drilling could be inserted in that sentence.)

Air quality in the Dallas–Fort Worth metroplex is poor. The region has consistently been characterized by the U.S. Environmental Protection Agency as a "non-attainment area," with levels of air pollution exceeding limits specified by the National Ambient Air Quality Standards. Though vehicle emissions are a significant source of air pollution in the metroplex, much of the pollution comes from industrial activities, including natural gas extraction (Armendariz 2009; Baker and Pring 2009).

Air emissions at natural gas sites come from two sources: direct and fugitive emissions from the gas well and from other pollutants onsite (such as diesel engines or open pits) (McKenzie et al. 2012). Methane is occasionally vented from the well directly into the air. Pressure on valves is released, and the valves sometimes leak. Engine exhaust is a major source of air-polluting emissions. Not only are there hundreds of diesel trucks traveling to and from a site, but many of the sites have combustion engines that run 24 hours per day to keep equipment operating. Open-air storage pits for a variety of fluids (such as drilling mud and flowback) are another source of air-polluting emissions.

Methane is a powerful greenhouse gas, and significant amounts of it are released into the atmosphere during gas-extraction activities (Howarth, Santoro, and Ingraffea 2011). Fugitive emissions of methane occur at several points in the extraction and transport of the gas. The highest percentage of the total comes during the flowback and drill-out phases. In addition, "a typical well has 55 to 150 connections to equipment such as heaters, meters, dehydrators, compressors, and vapor-recovery apparatus," and "many of these potentially leak, and many pressure relief values are designed to purposefully vent gas" (ibid., 683). Venting may be either a routine or an accidental practice. Howarth et al. calculate that, on average, between 3.6 percent and 7.9 percent of the total production of each individual well escapes into the atmosphere as methane.

These fugitive emissions may be also be contributing to global climate change. Molecule by molecule, methane is 72 times as powerful a greenhouse gas as carbon dioxide (Charman 2010). In the presence of sunlight and gaseous hydrocarbons, some of the pollutants associated with natural gas extraction, including nitrogen dioxide and volatile organic compounds, react to form ozone (Davis 2002).

"Red days"—days on which, according to the EPA's Air Quality Index, pollution is so bad that people should stay indoors—are common in the Dallas–Fort Worth metroplex, particularly in the summer months. There has even been an alarming instance of a "purple day" (American Lung Association 2011). Yet the public does not seem to have a good grasp of just how bad the air in this area is. In a study of Dallas residents, researchers found that the further people lived from the city center, the less likely they were to perceive air pollution as a problem (Brody, Peck, and Highfield 2004). People typically believe that the suburban and rural areas have the better air quality. Unfortunately, this is not the case, and air monitors in Keller and Denton (outer suburbs of the metroplex) record some of the worst pollution levels in the area. Residents sampled in the Dallas study also said they thought that air quality was much better in Texas than in other places in the United States, which is, of course, not always the case. "In many instances," Brody et al. write, "Texans tend to identify more strongly with their state than with a specific city or neighborhood." This "strong affinity with Texas," they comment, "reduces the distinction between local and state perceptions, but intensifies the distinction between state and other areas when it comes to rating air quality" (ibid., 1571). Other social factors also seemed to influence perceptions of air quality. Older people and those who were less politically conservative didn't think the air quality in the metroplex was as good as younger people and those who were more conservative thought it was. Both of these demographic characteristics—overall younger and politically conservative—represent the majority of the population in the areas in the metroplex with the most gas development.

Decades of research suggest that there is no threshold below which air pollution does not have a negative effect on health. Air pollution is associated with a host of ailments. "This relationship," Davis (2002, 232) writes, "has been found so often in so many places that it is no longer debated." And not only do the most polluted areas warrant concern; long-term, low-dose exposures to air pollution can be just as dangerous (and perhaps more insidious, because such pollution is less visible) as short-term, high-dose exposures (Goodell 2007, 124).

Researchers have identified higher than expected rates of asthma and other respiratory ailments in the Dallas–Fort Worth metroplex than in other areas of the state. The Cook Children's Community-Wide Children's Health Assessment and Planning Survey (2009) found that 17.5 percent of the children living in Denton County and 18.6 percent of those in Tarrant Country—among the counties with the most natural gas wells in the Barnett Shale—have been diagnosed with asthma (versus 14.3 percent of children statewide).

One activist, a woman in her early forties, told me that she believed there was a direct link between gas drilling and her respiratory problems. She developed asthma two years before our interview and now uses a rescue inhaler every day. "For someone who's never had breathing problems, it's scary," she said. "I just had my stress test, and my cholesterol's good and they told me I have a heart of a twenty-one-year-old, and I am a relatively healthy person. But for this. And it's really escalated. In fact, when I leave [the interview], my doctor wants me to do a pneumonia vaccination because he's very concerned. There are mornings I wake up and I'm like [feigns gasping for breath]. My doctor says there is a huge increase in adult asthma."

Many of the activists I spoke with mentioned the high rates of asthma in the Dallas–Fort Worth area. They and/or their children have been diagnosed with asthma. They attribute asthma flare-ups to activities at the gas wells.

One activist mentioned that a state regulator had come to her home to investigate her complaint about odors at a gas well located on her property. "The TCEQ investigator, in the investigation report, said the emissions made him ill," she said. But the investigator could leave the premises. She, in contrast, lives next to the well. Smell alone is likely to raise alarm and create psychological distress in people within proximity, even when the odors are said to be harmless.

Another activist summed up her feelings about gas-extraction activities and air pollution this way:

TCEQ for instance has a permit level where it's like twenty-five tons per year they can pollute with VOCs. And I figured it out at one point. Just to pollute five tons per year would've been like the equivalent of going outside every single day, dumping three and a half gallons of gasoline on the ground, and just let it evaporate. Every day. Can you imagine, if you did that at your house, how unpleasant it would be at your neighbor's house? Now multiple that times five and that's what the state will allow.

Water Pollution

As is documented in the film *Gasland*, people whose well water has been contaminated with natural gas can hold a cigarette lighter to a running tap and flames will shoot out across the room.

"One of the coolest things I've seen," one activist told me, "is natural gas bubbling up in a horse pasture. When it rained it would create these puddles and it would bubble up. You could light it on fire." She also told me about a similar phenomenon she claimed to have witnessed at a home she had visited:

Weird stuff started happening, like water would seep up and it would be oily. Their dogs would drink it—it would just seep up. Their dogs would drink this water and would get bloody vomiting and diarrhea. [The homeowner] would find a spot where it was dry. She'd dig a hole. Within three of four minutes the water would seep up. It was the weirdest thing. Then her well water started foaming like dishwater.

Activists in the Barnett Shale are concerned about a variety of water-related issues, including discharges of pollutants into fresh water, the potential for contamination of aquifers, and the use of large quantities of water in fracking.

Approximately 35,000 natural gas wells are fracked in the United States each year. The EPA estimates that the water consumed to frack these wells is equivalent to the amount of water consumed by 5 million people in a year (Schmidt 2011). An estimated 5 million or more gallons of water are used each day by natural gas companies in the Barnett Shale. According to Andrews, Folger, and Humphries (2009, 24), "wells subject to multiple treatments consume several million gallons of water. An Olympic-size swimming pool (164 ft × 82 ft × 6 ft deep) holds over 600,000 gallons of water, for comparison, and the average daily per capital consumption of fresh water (roughly 1,420 gallons per day) is 522,000 gallons over one year." This finding is particularly poignant in Texas, where drought is common. North Texas counties consistently have had burn bans in effect because of dry conditions and have received recent disaster declarations for fire and drought effects on farmland. Water rationing is routine, with restrictions for use watering lawns and gardens. One study found that water use in the Dallas–Fort Worth metroplex caused the water in the Trinity Aquifer (the major aquifer in North Texas) to drop more than 500 feet (ibid.). As a result, some rural towns on the outskirts of the metroplex have run out of water during the summer months.

"We do know from open records," an activist told me, "that in the four county Upper Trinity Groundwater Conservation District, in 2009 I think, [the gas industry used] two billion gallons of water from metered sources. There were many incidents where they were getting water from unmetered sources. Which they weren't supposed to do, but they did anyway. They had no enforcement action and no fine for that."

How much water is used by the gas industry is a matter of debate. Some companies connect directly into municipal water via fire hydrants. One activist recounted a conversation he had had with a city official about how the city monitored and recorded such use:

They're hooking their hoses up to our fire hydrants. And [a city official] said "There's these meters they're supposed to be using [to measure the amount of water used]." And I said "OK, so who's overseeing that they're hooking up the meter?" She said "They're supposed to be doing it." And I said "Well, so you're telling me it's an honor system?" And she says "Well, yes."

This activist documented accounts in which the meters were nowhere to be seen. The cost of unmetered water is shifted to the city (and thereby the taxpaying public).

The activists argue that when drilling companies connect to the fire hydrants, the water use is officially recorded as municipal use (i.e., residential and commercial) rather than industrial use, and that, as a result, when industry representatives display charts indicating that their water consumption is a small percentage of the total water consumption in a city, those figures are misleading. Is this claim true? I do not know. But the claim has become part of the Shale narrative, and with it comes further distrust of industry "facts."

North Texas is one of the largest population centers in the United States, with approximately 7 million people in the Dallas–Fort Worth metroplex. Most of the region's drinking water comes from human made lakes; however, some communities, particularly on the outer edges of the metroplex, rely on well water from the Trinity Aquifer, one of only seven major aquifers in the state.

"I'm concerned about groundwater and surface water," one activist told me. "I mean, we can't pollute downstream from us. Anything that runs off right here, we don't drink it but the people down there do. Dallas. What if we pollute Dallas' water? What are they going to do to us, you know?" He laughed after he said that, but his point was well taken. If drilling companies in his city pollute surface water (and they have; companies have been caught discharging used frack water directly into streams that flow into area drinking water lakes), the impact downstream could be devastating.

A research team identified four possible impacts of natural gas fracking on water supplies in Pennsylvania:

(*i*) fluid (water and gas) flow and discharge to shallow aquifers due to the high pressure of the injected fracturing fluids in the gas wells; (*ii*) the toxicity and radioactivity of produced water from a mixture of fracturing fluids and deep saline formation waters that may discharge to the environment; (*iii*) the potential explosion and asphyxiation hazard of natural gas; and (*iv*) the large number of private wells in rural areas that rely on shallow groundwater for household and agricultural use . . . that are typically unregulated and untested. (Osborn et al. 2011, 8172)

In their study of drinking-water wells near fracking operations in Pennsylvania, Osborn et al. (ibid.) found significantly higher levels of methane in the water wells closest to the natural gas wells. Out of a sample of 68 drinking-water wells, methane was identified in 51 (85 percent), with the highest concentrations in those wells closest to the gas wells. The average of these levels was below the "action level" for hazard mitigation designated by the U.S. Department of the Interior. The chemical signature of the methane found in these water wells was consistent with deep thermogenic methane rather than surface-level biogenic sources, signifying cross-contamination from the gas wells. The researchers hypothesized that either the wells' casings were leaky or the fractures might extend beyond the shale formation, allowing gas to migrate into the underground water supplies.

Whereas methane limits for explosion and asphyxiation hazards are well known, little scientific research has been conducted on the long-term health effects of methane exposure. There also has been little if any research on the effects of ingestion of methane after contamination of drinking water.

Between March 2009 and April 2011, the U.S. Environmental Protection Agency conducted an extensive study of water well complaints associated with natural gas drilling in Pavillion, Wyoming (DiGiulio et al. 2011). They found evidence of shallow groundwater contamination from fracking and from holding pits. The EPA and other regulatory agencies have documented water contamination caused by migration of natural gas into water wells and by overflow from pits and holding ponds into adjacent pasture or farm land (Rahm 2011). Liquid in open-air pits is free to evaporate into the air. The pits are lined with plastic, yet on many accounts they have leaked or overflowed. State officials in New Mexico have documented about 800 instances of water contamination due to oil and gas operations, about 400 of which were attributable to leaky waste pits (Charman 2010).

One activist told me that she had photographic documentation of hundreds of abandoned open-air pits. I saw some of her photographs.

"In Texas," she said, "you don't have to line or fence the pits. It is not a requirement. Now, in New Mexico, they had over four hundred cases of groundwater contamination that they traced back directly to the pits."

"That makes sense," I said. "If they are unlined."

"Right. Now, they have a pit rule in New Mexico. Only on very strict cases can they have a pit. They have to do a closed loop system. Guess how many cases of groundwater contamination they've had since then? Zero. I have 360 aerial photos and you can just see these pits everywhere. They're abandoned. Sometimes they'll line them, but the lining gets torn up and they just bury it. They don't remediate. They just bury it. It's like a toxic burrito. This one put right down from my house, not far, it was just 15 feet from a creek that flowed directly into Denton Creek. It was 15 feet from this creek. It was the nastiest mess. I actually trespassed and took a lot of photos of it."

Denton Creek eventually makes its way to Lake Lewisville, the source of drinking water for a large portion of the metroplex's population.

Another water-related concern in the Barnett Shale is the disposal of waste water. In the Barnett Shale, most waste water from the drilling of natural gas wells (including flowback from fracking) is eventually disposed of in deep injection wells.

"It's not clean water that's being injected. It's produced water," one activist told me.

"Do people worry it will seep into the aquifer?" I asked.

"I think that's definitely one of the primary concerns citizens have. We know you're injecting it, but what's happening during the process? Is it feasible that it could contaminate drinking water supplies? For the most part, North Texas relies on surface water for drinking [but] there are some private wells. It's more of a rural concern because the rural communities use more wells. But that's part of the debate. If the City of Fort Worth doesn't allow [injection wells] in the urbanized area, they've forced these wells to go out into the rural community. The rural community doesn't have as strong of a voice because there's not as many people. They're being forced to take disposal wells next to them because [people] don't want them in the city. Fundamentally, politically, how do you deal with that? That's a huge human importance issue. There are also concerns about injecting dirty, used, produced water into the ground again. What's going to happen to it?"

Water, produced water, waste water —water use is framed differently by different speakers. "I'm trying to discipline myself," one activist said, "to call it 'waste water.' They like calling it 'water' to make it sound inert. But it's . . . you don't want to drink it."

Another activist told me about problems a friend of hers was having with her water well. The friend, a woman in her seventies, lived next to a well pad. The activist explained:

She gets her drinking water from a well. It's a long story. She won't go against anything [the gas company] is doing, but she's living a nightmare. She said she'll get up, get in her car, when the fumes are so overpowering. She'll just drive to, like, Super Wal-Mart and walk the aisles for hours just to get away from here. She has to put earplugs in her ears and she has to take sleeping pills to sleep. Now she said she has a rash, all over her body, and she's been to doctors and she doesn't know what's causing it. I said, "Do you think it's your water?" and she said "Well, my son is telling me that the water's fine." She had to sign her property over to her kids. It's a long story, but for legal reasons, so she doesn't have ownership, but she lives there. It's been her house. Her son told her not to make waves. So she does what her son tells her and I kind of wonder if it's not from the water.

Wondering whether people have been exposed to something toxic is a theme that runs through the discourse of the Barnett Shale. Another activist told me about a water-related pollution event that focused her attention on water contamination issues. Someone she knew had "bubbling frack fluid in her yard." The fluid was flammable, suggesting methane contamination. Members of the family suffered frequent, painful rashes and other health problems.

One significant difficulty with regulating water use and pollution centers on the question of who *owns* the water. Water rights are a murky issue in Texas, which boasts a population of more than 26 million people (and is experiencing considerable population growth) in combination with year after year of drought. "The unanswered question," Yardley writes (2001), "is whether all this activity will skew who gets water and who does not in the future, or influence how much it will cost." Many researchers predict water shortages in the state are a coming crisis. "If the wars of this century were fought over oil," Ismail Serageldin, vice president of the World Bank, reportedly said in 1995 (as cited in Shiva 2002, ix), "the wars of the next century will be fought over water."

Shiva (2002, ix) describes "clashes of water cultures," some of which view water as sacred, some of which view it as a commodity, and some of which view it as free and abundant. Control over water signifies significant power. In a power struggle over water, it is typically the poor and disenfranchised who will lose. Control of water supplies coupled with pollution of water sources, Shiva writes, amounts to corporate terrorism. As of this writing there is little control over water supplies in Texas, but a lot of water is used there.

"A country," Shiva writes (2002, 1), "is said to be facing a serious water crisis when available water is lower than 1,000 cubic meters per person per year. Below that point, the health and economic development of a nation are considerably hampered. When the annual water availability per person drops below 500 cubic meters, people's survival is grievously compromised." Shiva herself saw the streams near her home dry up as a result of mining activities. Towns in the Barnett Shale that rely on well water from the aquifer have periodically run out of water too. Current levels of water use in North Texas are not sustainable.

Food and Soil Contamination

"I was driving down I-35 the other day towards Fort Worth, and right across from [landmark] there's a well right now that they're drilling," one activist told me. "There was a bunch of dark smoke coming out. So I was like 'What's that?' I drove around and looked. Just off the highway, it's a little dirt road. It was past the gas well. The gas well itself wasn't the problem. I went back and followed the road and came to this huge compressor area [the source of the smoke]. And right across the street was a house, a home, and it had a big For Sale sign in front of it. They had a beautiful orchard. They had this sign like a 'come and pick' thing. I don't know. How can you live next to something like that?" Many of the activists I interviewed expressed concerns about ground and food contamination and mentioned cattle grazing near gas operations, spills, and other contamination issues.

Through a process known as biomagnification, those at the top of the food chain end up with a greater concentration of a particular chemical within their systems. When we eat an animal, we also eat all the chemicals that have accumulated in that animal's flesh. Another activist told me a story about a man she knew who had purchased a piece of property in the northwestern Dallas–Fort Worth region and had begun to raise grass-fed, organic beef cattle. He later learned that the property next to his was the site of a deep injection well used for the disposal of waste water from gas drilling, and he began to worry about how that might affect his cattle. The activist told me that she purchases local, organic foods as much as she can. She wondered whether she was eating contamination from the wells, and, if so, how that might affect her.

"I've seen cattle drinking out of pits," another respondent told me. "I sent a video of it to the Texas Southwestern Cattle Association. Got an angry email back, 'cattle will not drink drilling waste.' I have pictures. [The cattle] like the salt. I see these baby calves all the time licking the pipes . . . because they like the salt. So they get the benzene, and the benzene's sweet. They get the benzene and the radiation and everything else that comes with it. And then we eat them."

That activist also told me of a peach orchard contaminated by overflow from a flowback pit and claimed that the industry had paid off the owner to dispose of the peaches. She claimed that in such cases it is stipulated that the people not talk publicly about what happened. (Hence my inability to corroborate the story.) As with many of the "facts" of the Shale narrative, however, whether true or not, the stories themselves are in the collective imagination. Told and retold, they shape the social representation. The fear of contamination is real and has an influence on people's actions.

Cancer

Sheree had recurring swollen lymph nodes under her left armpit. She was only 26 years old, and her doctor had told her not to worry. Her intuition told her otherwise, and she had a nagging feeling that something was seriously wrong. One evening, lying on her son's bed reading him a story, she happened to rest her hand across her chest and felt a hard bump on the edge of her left breast. She says she knew it was cancer. She just knew.

Sheree bolted for the bathroom and raised her shirt in front of the mirror. She could see the outline of the tumor beneath her skin.

The next day, Sheree made an appointment with her doctor, who saw her right away. After two mammograms and a sonogram, an oncologist came into the exam room, handed her a business card, and said "Here's my cell phone number. Call me any time if you need it. You're young. There's treatments. You just keep smiling your pretty smile."

Sheree was stunned.

She did not make a connection between her cancer and natural gas drilling right away, and she says she's still not 100 percent sure that's what caused it. Insight into the possibility happened serendipitously, when an acquaintance mentioned that a compression facility was going up near their homes.

Sheree didn't think about the health implications; she worried about the value of her property. That was a legitimate concern. Oil and gas facilities have significant negative effects on property values. One research team found that within a 2½-mile radius around oil and gas operations, property values are reduced by 4–8 percent on average, the amount of the reduction could be even higher depending on the intensity of industrial activity (Boxall et al. 2005). Such an impact on property values translates not only into a dip in home sales, but also into declines in school and property-tax revenues.

Sheree began to research compression stations, and she came across information about the negative health effects, including information about toxic compounds at natural gas sites and their potential to cause cancer.

There already were some gas pads near Sheree's home—some of the oldest pads in the area. Through an open records search, Sheree discovered that the pad closest to her home had had a faulty cement casing. An older well, records indicated there had been multiple toxic releases from the site and that the well had undergone prolonged flaring in the early days of its operation.

Sheree also discovered she was not the only young woman in her neighborhood with breast cancer. In fact, there were so many that one of them decided to form a support group. Nearly all of them had been less than 40 years old when diagnosed.

Sheree is in remission now, and her outlook is good. She lives in the same home. She worries that the cancer may return. She worries about the health of her family. And she wonders if she and her neighbors developed cancer as a result of that problematic natural gas well.

It is extremely difficult to identify a direct cause of cancer. "Because cancer is produced by so many things that do not leave any special marks on their victims," Davis (2002, xv) writes, "the medical community can rarely pinpoint the causes of any one person's illness. People lead complicated lives, pay mortgages, move, marry, divorce, and do many other things that make it challenging to figure out why they became sick." Connecting a cancer diagnosis to a specific environmental exposure is exceedingly difficult. Too many overlapping, interacting variables are involved.

While examining patterns of cancer in their city, some residents of the Town of Flower Mound (located between Dallas and Fort Worth) felt that they had enough evidence to support claims that natural gas drilling was increasing the incidence of cancer in their neighborhoods. They asked the Texas Department of State Health Services (DSHS) to intervene. The DSHS investigated all leukemia subtypes (in adults and in children), all cases of breast cancer, and all cases of childhood brain and central nervous system cancer in Flower Mound. Data from tumor-registry data were used in the analysis. The investigators found "a slight elevation of female breast cancer," and reported "a statistically significant elevation was found among females for breast cancer" in two ZIP codes in Flower Mound (DSHS 2010, 1). In ZIP code 75028, for the years 1998–2007, the observed number of breast cancer cases was 183, with an expected number of 134.0, placing the standardized incident ratio (the number of observed cases divided by the number of expected cases) at 1.4 ($p < 0.01$), standardized for both age and race. In the combined ZIP codes of 75022 and 75028, the observed number of cases was 251, with an expected count of 193.3, placing the standardized incident ratio at 1.3 ($p < 0.01$). These figures indicate that levels of breast cancer in these ZIP codes are statistically significantly higher than they should be.

Although the DSHS investigators identified a problem in Flower Mound, they did not attempt to explain *why* this was happening. "Because of the inherent limitations associated with these types of investigations," they wrote in their report, "we cannot determine with any degree of certainty why the number of breast cancer cases is higher than expected." (DSHS 2010, 1)

Both the investigation and the final report generated a lot of attention in the news media and in social networking. What did the results mean for the residents of those ZIP codes, and for the surrounding areas? Was benzene from natural gas drilling causing cancer? The investigation offered little in the way of answers. The DSHS reported that it would continue to monitor cancers rates in Flower Mound. But the residents wanted to see some action.

In 2011, a local news outlet reported that invasive breast cancer was on the rise across North Texas and linked the increase to natural gas drilling. "According to the Texas Commission on Environmental Quality's 2010 inventory of gas production equipment in the 24 counties of the Barnett Shale," the author states at the end of the article (Heinkel-Wolfe 2011), "the same six counties with rising rates of invasive breast cancer also have the highest count of compressors, separators, tanks and other above-groups points of emissions." Many of the residents were upset by the "wait and see" approach taken by the state. If cancer rates were problematic in the town, they believed the state should do something about it.

Whether or not the increase in breast cancer is in fact attributable to drilling, the connection is being actively constructed in the discourse, and those links are being made in the social representation. According to the Thomas Theorem, things that are believed to be real are real in their consequences. Connections between gas drilling and illness in discursive practice construct and objectify the social representation of gas drilling as a community health threat.

Investigations of cancer clusters in Texas are typically prompted by complaints from citizens. Citizens perceive what they believe to be an excess of cancer cases in their area, and they seek to find a common cause. Calls for cancer cluster studies reflect people's fear of cancer (Aldrich and Sinks

2002) and their response to ambient stressors. When confronted with cancer diagnoses, many people seek to learn the cause. Why did they get this disease? Knowing the cause may serve to externalize responsibility—"It was not my fault that I got cancer." This knowing also serves to quell the fears of the people who are well—"If I know the cause of someone else's cancer, I can avoid that cause and protect myself." Unfortunately, cancer cluster studies seldom uncover any useful information about the causes and prevention of cancer (ibid.). This is not to say that such studies have never been useful; it is simply to say that the percentage of investigations in which a common cause was confirmed is quite low. As I have already mentioned, there are so many variables when it comes to cancer that it is exceedingly difficult for epidemiologists to proclaim "Aha! I know what caused your cancer!" They are much more likely to scratch their heads and say they don't really know.

When done properly, cancer cluster investigations are both time intensive and resource intensive. As people increasingly recognize possible connections between cancer and toxins in the environment, community members have called for an increasing number of such investigations. These investigations consume a large amount of public health resources (Bellec, Hemon, and Clavel 2005). Because their resources are limited, public health departments must prioritize the intensity of these investigations. Often the community does not recognize how long it takes to conduct an adequate investigation (Williams et al. 2002). This should be communicated at the onset of the investigation, along with a reasonable explanation of what the investigation can accomplish (ibid.). Unfortunately, information about the process and what it might uncover was not adequately communicated during the Flower Mound investigation, and there was a disconnection between investigation of the cluster and community expectations related to the outcome.

"So what did they do," I asked an activist during an interview, "when they found there is a breast cancer cluster?"

"They are not calling it a cluster," the interviewee replied. "What they are saying ..."

"They found some breast cancer they didn't expect," I interjected.

"Higher than expected incidence of breast cancer in Flower Mound." Indeed, the DSHS report specifically does not identify the increases in breast cancer in Flower Mound as a "cancer cluster." This is in contrast to the perception of many Flower Mound residents that cancer rates are rampant in their town:

One of the gentlemen who was involved with us early on, he had a child with leukemia. And then all of a sudden you met another mom with a child with leukemia. And another. And then one of our friends who was an activist last year, her grandson was diagnosed. And he's still going through treatments.

It is certainly possible that the "cluster" (or, as the Texas Department of State Health Services would have it, the excess of cases) in Flower Mound is a statistical anomaly. Geographic clusters of disease do happen solely by chance. This is particularly the case with more common conditions, such as breast cancer or leukemia. Nonetheless, members of the community perceive a danger. "It is nearly impossible to prove that a particular person's cancer results from a particular chemical," writes Nichols (2008, 128), "at least in terms of the standards of legal proof. It is also difficult to determine, within the limits of scientific inquiry, whether a particular individual's cancer results from a particular exposure."

"We've had three separate 'looks,' if you will, in Flower Mound," an activist told me:

The first had to do with thyroid cancer. The second, they came in to investigate at the request of moms whose kids were diagnosed [with leukemia]. And while they were looking at the leukemia, they noticed that we had higher than expected rates of breast cancer. The leukemia moms were ticked off. They feel not all cases were considered. They [DSHS] tried to wash it away, but at least with the moms, they still weren't satisfied. I guess with them it's a gut feeling. So . . . what should I say about it? The numbers seem high. I'm not a statistician, so I can't talk to you about how they look at things. I will just say that some of the people that I know continue to have concerns and it seems like frequently there are new cases coming up.

There was a clear difference between how the activists assumed a cancer cluster investigation was performed and the actual methodology used by the state. The DSHS doesn't "come in" to investigate. Rather, in Texas, investigators conduct statistical analyses of data from the state's tumor registry. Physicians who diagnose a new tumor are required by law to report it to the registry (although there is no real penalty for not reporting). Disease surveillance systems of this kind are notoriously problematic because not all cases of a particular disease get reported. Reports may be missing information, and those reports will either be left as they stand, with incomplete data fields, or followed up on by a disease investigator, who may or may not be able to get the missing information. There can also be long lags in the accumulation of the data, including time between onset of illness and diagnosis of the cancer and time between diagnosis and complete reporting to the registry. Disease surveillance systems can tell us a lot about morbidity and mortality in a community, but they have real limitations due to data problems.

Activists criticized the state's methodology. They said that the geographic area utilized for the analysis (aggregated at the ZIP-code level) was too large. Activists argued that the cases of cancer in Flower Mound are concentrated in certain areas within the ZIP codes, but that information is washed out as a result of ZIP-code aggregation. They produced a map of known cases to demonstrate this point, but they said that their findings were discounted by the state.

"Instead of taking the two ZIP codes for Flower Mound, when you actually focus on the bulk of the cases, and the fact that they are in close proximity to each other, it's an added level of concern," an activist involved in the mapping project said. Activists were also concerned that not all of the cases were counted. This is a legitimate criticism of tumor registries.

Another problem the activists identified with the state's investigation was the lack of explanation as to why breast cancer rates were higher than expected. This was probably the most disconcerting facet of the process for them. Even though the activists found problems with the study's methodology, DSHS investigators still found higher incidence of breast cancer than would be expected in an average population. There must be some reason why. "I think it's important to note that the explanation they gave for that," one activist said. "Is it that, well, Flower Mound is an affluent community, so more women get mammograms?" She didn't buy the explanation, though. Statistically speaking, that should have been controlled for in the calculations, as they compare the rate of actual cases to the expected rate of cases in that geographic area, using data from that area. Thus, variation due to affluence should be controlled for. "None of the breast cancers were found through mammograms," the activist added. "They are all young women. Young women. So that doesn't fly." (Women under age 40 typically do not receive routine mammograms.)

In the end, the questions the state agency's investigation raised may have exceeded the answers it provided. Even if they *only* have a higher than expected incidence of breast cancer, the activists are concerned that no one is doing anything about it.

The story of natural gas development is ongoing. New data and research about health and safety related to natural gas development are released frequently. It is difficult to separate fact from speculation, and, as will be discussed later, facts are mutable. Meanwhile, communities involved are engaged in meaning-making activities, and their discursive practices build a collective representation of natural gas drilling as a threat to the health of the community's members.

"Each of us carries a lifetime of chemical exposures that we squire around each day," writes Nichols (2008, 101). "Some of these chemicals persist in our body for decades, and some of them are passed from generation to generation." Chemicals affect the human body at different dosages—some at high dosages, some at minute ones. Some have little effect at one dosage, yet are deadly at another (and such dosages are not always intuitive—some chemicals are more harmful at *smaller* dosages). Some are passed across the placenta. Some will lie dormant until activated by another chemical. Some will encourage growth of tumors already present in the body. Some will suppress the immune system. Some will kill—but who, and when? If this place is contaminated, why aren't more people sick? Why these particular people? Why not lots of people?

"I've seen clusters of illness here," one activist told me. When I asked what sorts of illnesses, she mentioned headaches, nosebleeds, thyroid problems, chronic fatigue, anemia, and cancer. These conditions come up repeatedly in the Shale discourse.

"What are they putting into the air?" the aforementioned activist asked me, visibly frustrated. "I'm so upset because I feel this is something I have no control over. If I'm a nonsmoker and I'm out in public, I can choose not to sit in the smoking area. But what do I do if this is my house? This is my property?" This feeling, a lack of control, seemed to create high levels of stress among the activists. Engaging in activism functioned to return some semblance of control to them.

4 A Lack of Competent Guardians

After a city council meeting, Jennifer and I meet at Starbucks to talk about the impact of natural gas drilling in her neighborhood. Jennifer is a small, unimposing woman who often wears her salt-and-pepper hair pulled back in a loose bun. Despite appearances, she's a powerhouse in the activist world. I like to watch her politely tell the politicians what needs to be done. She doesn't let them see her anger. Instead she presents fact after fact, trying to win them over with data. She carries notebooks filled with charts, graphs, tables, maps to all of the meetings. Though she doesn't let the politicians see her anger, she is filled with rage about the drilling.

"I'm having a real struggle living with this industry that has encroached upon our land here," Jennifer says. She tells me that she grew up in an industrial area on the Gulf Coast, near the refineries. She remembers the smell of the pollution. One of the draws of retiring to the city in which she now lives was that it is a bedroom community with lots of parks and other green spaces, trees, and wildflowers in the spring. When she purchased her home, there was little commerce and no industrial areas in her city.

"It's really hard. It's very stressful," she says. "It's like torture sometimes. You know, you have no control and you feel helpless. And we don't really have the city backing us up. It's all—let's be good neighbors with [the gas companies]. They are not good neighbors, guys! They are your worst enemy!" Jennifer has developed significant neurological problems that she attributes to the gas drilling in her neighborhood. She does not understand why, despite her ample evidence, the city council continues to side with the industry and allow gas development to continue to increase in the city.

Most of the activists I spoke with expressed similar feelings of hopelessness, and the sentiment runs through the Shale narrative. After identifying what they believe to be a threat both to their own health and to the health of the community, community members nearly always turn to a governmental agency for support. They are stunned to find that help is not forthcoming. Their sense of the proper role of the government—to protect the people—is violated, and they feel betrayed.

Natural gas companies enjoy a tremendous amount of political and legal power. Most aspects of natural gas operations operate outside of federal laws that would provide greater public-health protection. According to Colborn et al. (2011) and Tuhus (2011), they are excluded from or exempted from the Clean Water Act, the Clean Air Act, the Comprehensive Environmental Response, Compensation, and Liability (Superfund) Act, the Resource Conservation and Recovery Act, the Toxic Release Inventory (under the Emergency Planning and Community Right-to-Know Act), the National Environmental Policy Act, and the Safe Drinking Water Act.

The National Energy Policy Act of 2005 (passed during the George W. Bush administration) specifically exempted the practice of hydraulic fracturing from the Safe Drinking Water Act (Rahm 2011). This exemption is often referred to as the "Halliburton Loophole." At that time, Vice President Dick Cheney sat on the energy task force that crafted this legislation. Before taking office, Mr. Cheney was CEO of Halliburton—the company that perfected the fracking process. Many commentators argue that, through this and other connections, the oil and gas industry exerted a tremendous amount of influence over the actions of the energy task force (ibid.), and in the process managed to avert federal intervention in their practices.

In keeping with the Republican Party's ethos of small government, the gas industry as a whole has been deregulated. With little government oversight, the industry is required to monitor itself. As recently as the 1970s, natural gas was considered a public utility and was regulated as such, but that is no longer the case. One unintended consequence of deregulation is that consumers are exposed to increasingly wild market swings (Deffeyes 2005, 80). The public must also trust the industry to police itself.

I use the blanket term "the industry" throughout this book, but it is important to note that natural gas activities are not a cohesive whole and that not all of the employees working in the natural gas industry hold the same opinions on environmental issues. When most activists speak of the industry, they include not just the natural gas companies themselves, but also the roughnecks in the field, the engineers, and office workers, as well as the lobbyists, industry supporters, affiliated companies and organizations, the mineral owners who profit at the expense of property owners, the legislators who support deregulation, and so forth. Companies vary in their support for environmental protections and for public concern about the health and safety of their operations. The industry is not monolithic, but the goals and pursuits of its members align on the idea of—as one activist is fond of putting it— "Drill, baby, drill!" The industry is a conglomeration of power that is exceedingly difficult to oppose.

Mineral Rights and Surface Rights

Without federal regulation, responsibility for protection of health and the environment falls to the states. Generally speaking, state law prioritizes mineral extraction and revenue generation (Colborn et al. 2011). This is certainly the case in Texas. Ownership of mineral rights—that is, who owns any below-ground natural resources—varies from state to state. In Texas, property rights and mineral rights are typically severed. The purchaser of a home usually signs a waiver acknowledging that only surface rights are being purchased. Everything underground is owned by someone else. When natural gas is discovered on the property, this severing often leads to conflicts between the owner of the mineral rights and the owner of the surface rights.

When companies want to drill for natural gas on the property, the owners of the mineral rights often lease those rights to a gas company in exchange for royalty payments on any gas from the land that the company sells. Natural gas drilling takes place on both private and public (government-owned) lands. Royalty payments for leases range between 12.5 percent and 20 percent of the profits. Thus, mineral owners stand to make a sizable amount of money from leasing their minerals to the gas companies. Significantly, the government may also profit from gas development on public lands. Schmidt (2011, 349) writes:

the experience of Fort Worth—the epicenter of so-called urban drilling in the United States—offers a glimpse of the emerging issues and public debates around fracking. A fast-growing city of nearly 750,000 people, Fort Worth sits directly atop the Barnett Shale, where nearly 14,000 shale gas wells have been drilled since the late 1990s. Residents who own mineral rights to their property can sell leases to the gas industry for prices that range from hundreds to tens of thousands of dollars per acre, not to mention 18 percent or more in royalty payments on production.

Most often in Texas, however, the mineral rights are owned by someone other than the surface-property owner.

Conflicts arise when the owners of mineral rights want to get to the minerals but do not own the surface rights. This is particularly problematic when the minerals lie beneath a pre-existing structure. By Texas law, mineral owners must be allowed access to their minerals, which means they can come on to property owned by someone else to do so, and the property owner may not legally deny them access. The mineral owner is not financially responsible for property damage that occurs during this process, nor must they pay for the use of the land. Some states require compensation of the property owner for access to the minerals; however, this is not the case in Texas. One property owner I spoke with decried that she must pay property taxes for land that was completely unusable and inaccessible to her because it had been overtaken by a gas company (she does not hold any mineral rights), yet this is a typical practice in Texas. Rahm (2011, 2979) notes correctly that in Texas "mineral rights owners can use as much surface land as is reasonably necessary to explore, drill, and extract minerals. The mineral rights owner is allowed by Texas law to clear trees and remove fences so that drilling rigs can be brought to the property." This can involve use of one or more acres of land and includes the erection of distribution pipelines. It is against the law for an owner of surface rights to hinder this process.

In cases of pipeline construction, gas companies in Texas hold the legal authority of eminent domain, and for the most part they may lay pipe wherever they deem fit (Rahm 2011). This includes laying pipe on and across private property without the property owner's consent.

Mineral owners can lease their minerals to a gas company for both exploration and development. The lease is a contract between the mineral owner and the gas company that gives the gas company the right to extract and sell the gas in exchange for a percentage of the profits. Activists often call this income "mailbox money." The companies typically pay a "signing bonus" and then a set percentage of profits based on acreage. This money goes to the mailbox of the mineral owner, not to the property owner.

Some mineral owners, particularly those who own smaller plots, have said that they felt tricked into signing leases with the companies. Some homeowners who own all or part of their mineral rights say they did not fully understand the implications of signing the lease. They did not understand just how disruptive the drilling would be. I spoke with a woman who owns 50 percent of the mineral rights under her small yard about a meeting she attended during which a representative of a gas company explained leasing and asked everyone in her neighborhood to sign on with the company. Everyone in the neighborhood was given $1,500 to sign the contract. "Man, these people were lined up!" the woman said. "You were in this long, long line and you were just going in like cattle and they had you sign. And they said don't worry about reading the contract. Well, I guess you could have but there were so many people in line in back of you. . . . They were just getting people through. Just sign here. So we signed on the dotted line and off we went." Once the neighbors had signed the leasing agreements, a natural gas pad with eight wells was built on the site. The woman said that the residents did not understand the magnitude of the disruption that would happen to their neighborhood. "I knew nothing before all this," she said. "So [one night] at 3:30 in the morning, we're sleeping, we're awakened in the middle of the night. Banging, clanging. We hear trucks, you know that beep, beep! We hear this. Now we're two blocks away [from the site]. I hear a man on a loudspeaker like a foreman or something, talking to his employees at 3:30 in the morning! And they're operating like it's the middle of the day. OK? So that was like how this whole thing started."

Since receiving the original signing bonus, this woman hasn't received any money from her lease. She signed to receive less than 0.0123 percent of the profits based on the size of her property and her half of the rights. Once her portion reaches $100, she anticipates receiving about $10 per month.

Perhaps not surprisingly, property rights are a large theme in the discourse of natural gas drilling. "I thought this was America," said one activist. "I thought in America you had property. That they couldn't take this away." Yet both the industry and government regulators repeatedly violated people's assumptions about the rights and roles of the various entities involved. Homeowners understandably assumed that the property they had purchased, on which they lived, belonged to them, that they had say over what happened on their land. They assumed that any threat to their land would be prevented and protected by the government. They were wrong on both counts.

"All of the laws are set up to protect the industry," one activist told me. "It is organized crime. It is legal, organized crime. It's the Big Gas Mafia."

Another activist, with active, unwanted drilling on her property, said this: "You could argue that this is a violation of our Constitutional rights. I mean, it's almost like we're going back to the beginnings of our country. [The mineral owner], he's the king, and we're the servants, and he can come . . . he can hire a company to come on to my land, destroy it, and jeopardize the health and safety of my family." Perhaps not surprisingly, this created a tremendous feeling of helplessness and betrayal.

The aforementioned activist told me about her efforts to track down the mineral owner to see if she could appeal to him directly for protections for her family. Perhaps, she thought, the mineral owner was unaware of how drilling on her property was affecting her family. Through a time-consuming search of public records, she found the man who owned the minerals beneath her land. She discovered that he owned more than a thousand acres of minerals in the area around her home, and that he had leased all but a radius of 50 acres around his own home. She could not believe he would protect his own family and not anyone else. At first she thought this must be a mistake; that he simply did not know about the other families living on the surface of his minerals. Perhaps he didn't know the extent of disruption drilling was having on her family, with three gas wells on her five-acre property, and perhaps he would help her. "I sent him pictures of my daughter," she told me. "I sent certified letters. It was like, how could you . . . ? I cannot believe it."   .

Nothing was done.

The activist also reached out repeatedly to state and local regulatory agencies for help. "If you had told me all this two years ago, before all this started, I would not have believed you. I would have said they're state agencies, they are paid for by my tax dollars. They would help me. They would not, absolutely never let half of this go on." She says now that was a faulty assumption, and that she was betrayed by her own government.

Regulatory Agencies

To intercede on behalf of the public, a regulatory agency must have the legal authority to act. When it comes to the oil and gas industry—particularly in Texas—regulators have exceedingly little power. The laws are overwhelmingly supportive of the industry. In addition, what legal authority exists is largely fragmented between a number of organizations, and different agencies regulate different aspects of the process, which can be quite difficult to navigate. Yet these are the agencies to which the public turns when there is a problem. The public trusts that the government will be there to help them when something goes wrong. And when help is not forthcoming, there is a tremendous feeling of violation.

Referring to the Texas system as "the wild West," Rahm (2011) writes that "the fragmentation of the Texas regulatory bureaucracy, a fundamental anti-regulatory disposition of the TCEQ and the Governor, and the well-entrenched legal and administrative structures that promote oil and gas extraction above other concerns make Texas a strong pro-drilling state."

"Residents' lived experience is that of a complex entanglement of many interrelated problems," Gunter and Kroll-Smith (2007, 86) write, "but an agency's narrow and instrumental focus only on a subset of those problems means that in the very act of ameliorating some problems, it may unintentionally exacerbate others." Multiple agencies with multiple roles, in combination with no real legal power to intervene, in a contentious political climate—it is no wonder that some citizens feel exasperation. This perfectly describes what I found during this project.

The U.S. Environmental Protection Agency

The U.S. Environmental Protection Agency has authority over air, water, and soil quality, but there are many exemptions to its power. The EPA was founded in 1970 under President Richard Nixon. According to Goodell (2007, 127), "Nixon was no tree hugger ('You better watch out for those crazy enviros, Bill,' he warned EPA head Bill Ruckelshaus in 1972. 'They're a bunch of commie pinko queers!'), but he was a shrewd politician, and he understood very clearly that any political system that fails to protect the health and safety of its citizens will not survive long."

The EPA has very little legal authority to regulate natural gas development operations. The agency has been involved in conducting scientific studies on fracking and the EPA provides policy recommendations on oil and gas activities as related to the natural environment to the states. Because Texas politicians favor states' rights, they oppose most federal interventions. As a result the EPA and regulatory agencies in Texas seldom agree. Texas has brought lawsuits against the EPA many times (see, for example, Koffler 2012), and many conservatives in Texas believe that the EPA and other federal agencies interfere with economic growth and free enterprise in the states.

Residents often contact the EPA for assistance and are (correctly, according to jurisdictional authority) referred back to state regulatory agencies.

Texas Regulation

State laws provide regulation for issues that fall outside federal control (Rahm 2011). As such, laws can and do vary greatly from state to state. Owing to an ethos of individuality and states' rights, Texas oil and gas regulations are weak and are fragmented across a multitude of agencies and jurisdictions. The oil and gas industry, besides being an economic engine that keeps the state running, is a large part of Texas culture and heritage. The industry is entrenched in Texas politics. It is one of the state's most important industries—indeed, Texas is one of the largest producers of oil and gas in the world (ibid.).

Conservative Texas politics oppose federal intervention and favor states' rights. Governor Rick Perry had spoken of the possibility that Texas might secede from the United States (Huffington Post 2009), and in each legislative session there is inevitably a petition filled with signatures demanding such. At one time Texas was an independent republic, and some people in the state would like to return to that status.

The Texas Railroad Commission

The Texas Railroad Commission still regulates many aspects of the oil and gas industry. Its primary directive, to quote one Railroad Commission official I spoke with, is "to get the minerals out of the ground." (And natural gas is considered a mineral.) As was noted in chapter 1, oil once was shipped across the country—mainly out of Texas—on railroad tank cars, and the Railroad Commission obtained a significant amount of power as a result.

During the Great Depression, the Railroad Commission regulated national oil prices by limiting the amount of oil that left Texas (Deffeyes 2005, 44). In effect, it functioned as OPEC later would, limiting production and controlling oil prices.

The Railroad Commission often finds itself at odds with federal regulators. According to Childs (2005, 261), "the adversary relationship between state and national regulators and especially between producing and consuming states [has] resulted in a regulatory mess."

The Railroad Commission promotes natural gas development and sets standards for oil and gas permitting. The agency is not responsible for protection of human health or environmental concerns, nor has it been throughout its history. It is also important to note that many of the laws that govern the Railroad Commission were written with rural oil and gas development, rather than urban activities, in mind (Childs 2005).

The Texas Commission on Environmental Quality

The Texas Commission on Environmental Quality (TCEQ) is responsible for air and water quality in Texas—but not, as many believe, for the protection of human health, aside from how public health is impacted tangentially by environmental pollution problems. A major theme in the TCEQ's mission statement is that it will provide protection in ways "consistent with sustainable economic development" (TCEQ 2014). The economic-development portion of the TCEQ's mission is important because it pertains to the true ability of the TCEQ to intervene in pollution events—often it is unable to provide protection when to do so stands in the way of economic growth and profit.

Texas has historically been weak on environmental protections, taking the side of development and progress over conservation. And, like the Railroad Commission, the TCEQ has frequently clashed with the U.S. Environmental Protection Agency.

Formerly known as the Texas Natural Resource Conservation Commission, or TNRCC (which many environmentalists pronounced as "train wreck" as a slight on the agency's performance), the TCEQ was established by the Texas Legislature in 1993. Its name was changed to Texas Commission on Environmental Quality in 2001. Although the Texas government had a role in the protection of the environment before the 1990s, such regulation was dispersed into a number of both state and local agencies and advisory boards. These organizations were collected under the TCEQ umbrella. Establishment of the TNRCC consolidated various air-quality and water-quality activities along with regulation of waste management into one agency. Fewer than 3,000 employees cover the entire state, and 70 percent of those are headquartered in the main office in Austin. Their duties include responding to environmental complaints related to natural gas development along with all other environment-related complaints and a myriad of other duties.

Indeed, in the TCEQ's strategic plan (TCEQ 2013b) it is difficult to find much mention of work related to natural gas. This is not to suggest that the agency is not concerned about environmental pollution associated with the natural gas industry, but rather to demonstrate the diverse range of responsibilities the agency holds. Recently, TCEQ has increased ambient air monitoring in several areas in Texas with natural gas development activities in an attempt to quantify changes in air quality. The TCEQ is also responsive to citizens' complaints, although perhaps not to the extent those citizens might wish.

The TCEQ is relatively small, understaffed, and underfunded. Only a handful of investigators cover the entire Barnett Shale. In 2009, the lags between complaints about problems at natural gas sites and TCEQ investigations were so long that TCEQ rules were changed to require that an investigator be present at a gas site within 12 hours of a complaint. Nevertheless, trouble at a gas site may be over by the time the investigator arrives.

The TCEQ investigates about thirty Barnett Shale related complaints per month.

The Texas Department of State Health Services

The overarching mission of the Texas Department of State Health Services is to improve health and well-being in the state, and the agency oversees an enormous array of health-related activities.

When it comes to oil and gas operations, the DSHS's main mandate concerns naturally occurring radioactive material (NORM). The DSHS regulates the receipt, possession, storage, use, and treatment of NORM. The Railroad Commission regulates disposal of NORM related to oil and gas waste, and the TCEQ regulates all disposal of NORM except that associated with oil and gas. The variety of agencies involved in different aspects of this material demonstrates the fragmentation of Texas regulatory agencies.

Texas has little if any infrastructure for tracking environment-related health problems. In Texas, providers of health care are mandated to report occurrences of certain infectious diseases and of a few chronic diseases to the Texas Department of State Health Services, and those occurrences then are tracked by epidemiologists. No similar tracking system is in place for environmentally caused conditions (with the exception of lung disease resulting from exposure to asbestos). One branch of the Department of

State Health Services investigates suspected clusters of environmentally caused cancers or other disease clusters in a very limited way. Most of its investigations are prompted by requests from citizens rather than by anomalies detected in the course of routine surveillance.

Like many other agencies in Texas, the Department of State Health Services is fragmented into a number of branches, divisions, and regional offices. These components tend to be isolated in silos, which limits sharing of information.

County Authority

Of all the regulatory agencies, the county has the least legal authority over oil and gas development, yet people living in unincorporated areas of the state are likely to seek help from county officials. The main legal authority the county holds involves county-owned roads and bridges. The county also has limited jurisdiction over the routing of pipelines, primarily in relation to location permitting and plotting in unincorporated areas. This is to the detriment of residents of unincorporated areas.

"You can go out in the county, and they've got lines, flex lines, moving material from one pit to the next," one regulatory official told me. "They're just old irrigation lines, where you put them together and once the pressure gets good, you know, high enough, it will actually seal off. Well, if you've ever seen those work out in the field, well, you plug them into each other and you run your pressure and they leak like a sieve until they finally pressure up. Those things are all over the place out there. Material is being released as it's being moved around. There are fire hoses running everywhere. There's a lot of stuff going on out in the county. Things you wouldn't even think about. Like for example, they run [the lines] through culverts and such. Well, now you've reduced the capacity of your culverts. You have a storm and all of a sudden your culvert's plugged up with these lines and now you've got a localized flooding issue, plus the ability for that line to lose its integrity and release immediately into that storm water."

Whereas cities have some power to influence oil and gas activities in their jurisdictions, residents of unincorporated areas get little help in doing so. County officials have no say over hours of operation, noise control, or setbacks. (A setback is the distance between a gas pad and a home or some other structure.)

"What the drillers would do out in the county when nobody was watching," a city official told me, "that scared me."

In unincorporated areas, jurisdiction over most aspects of drilling falls back to the Railroad Commission. Residents are stuck with the Railroad Commission's minimum setback requirement of least 250 feet between the well (the actual hole in the ground) and the perimeter of a home. One belief I heard repeated often is that the 250-foot setback was delimited because 250 feet is the maximum height of an oil drill, so that the structure would not be destroyed if the drill were to topple over. County governments have no authority to expand setback requirements.

City Authority

Cities in Texas have some options for intervention between residents and the industry. They have limited capacity to regulate water quality, through ordinances for watershed protection and permits for activities within flood plains. They also can enact regulations about noise, lighting, and the aesthetics of a site, and can specify some requirements about the equipment itself (for instance, requiring that generators be run on electricity rather than diesel fuel). They can also require larger setbacks than the minimum set by the Railroad Commission. Municipalities do not have legal power to regulate air quality in Texas. That function is held by the state. Fire departments are involved in safety inspections and in planning for explosion disasters.

"Cities are a horrible place for a gas well, but the laws are favorable to industry," one city official told me in an interview. "The city has a limited ability to do some stuff [to control what happens at the site] but we can't legally stop it." Another official noted that, owing to myriad legal issues, there are many "complicated nuances of drilling in an urban environment." Many of the city officials I interacted with spoke of the need to overhaul of oil and gas legislation at the state level so as to take urban environments into account. Another official said this:

Any time you've got an issue where you don't have direct legislative supported regulatory authority by the state and you're attempting to introduce a standard that is more stringent than the state or federal standard then you immediately open yourself up for a preemptive challenge [lawsuit], the idea being that those standards are in place at the state and federal level to address those issues and therefore the local policy makers—the opinion is—they don't have a role in enforcing that particular issue.

Municipalities' fear of lawsuits was a repeated theme in my research. Though it could be argued that cities might face lawsuit from community members, the reality is that the industry has more funds (and a cadre of lawyers) with which to bring suit than the residents of a city have.

It is important to note that in Texas state-level legislation was enacted for *rural* oil and gas activities, and that Texas laws reflect this. Urban drilling, a recent phenomenon, was not among the original legislative considerations. Because of this legislative history, cities are forced to mediate between the desires of multiple constituents.

One activist summed up the role of Texas' cities this way:

I've thought about city ordinances, as if they were a soundboard. Like a sound engineer has all these knobs you can move up or down. Each of those tracks represents a particular line you can put in the ordinance. Like green completions, which the EPA [supports], so should we require green completions? If you move it up, it's increasing costs because it's increasing regulations and it's protecting health and the environment. So the battle is where to set those levels I think.

Because the Dallas–Fort Worth metroplex comprises hundreds of cities and towns, each of which can have a unique oil and gas ordinance, rules the cities implement for the gas industry are precarious—particularly along the borders. For example, one town in the Barnett Shale has a setback of 1,000 feet, which means that a natural gas well cannot be drilled within 1,000 feet of what is called a "Protected Use property," such as a house or a school or a hospital, or other designated facilities. This town issued a permit for the construction of a gas well right on the edge of the city limits. The road behind the property was the delimiter between this town and the neighboring town. Across that road was a preschool. The preschool was easily within 1,000 feet of the well, but it was in the neighboring town and thus the city's oil and gas ordinance did not protect it. The neighboring town also had an oil and gas ordinance that would have protected the preschool; however, the permit to drill the well was not in that town. This differentiation, from jurisdiction to jurisdiction, also creates confusion and frustration for residents.

911

Sometimes the public calls the emergency telephone number 911 in order to complain about problems at the sites of gas wells. Common stories from activists involve differential and inadequate 911 response. For example, one evening when a well vented because of a power outage, a number of residents called 911. The calls were routed to 911 dispatchers in two different cities. Dispatchers in the two cities gave very different information. One told residents not to worry, that it was "just air."

"One of my neighbors said when he called 911 they might as well have just hung up on him," one resident recalled. "He was terrified and was asking the operator, should he evacuate? And they were like 'I don't know, just do whatever you feel like you need to do.'" Meanwhile, the other city's dispatcher advised people about explosion hazards. That dispatcher reportedly told callers not to light matches, not to turn on their vehicles, and to take precautions. This divergent set of responses—one dispatcher telling callers not to worry while the other warned of explosion hazards—demonstrates difficulties that concerned residents face. Which direction should they follow? Who should they turn to for help?

"There's nobody you can call," one respondent told me. "I keep calling and 911 wouldn't do anything about the noise [from the well]. But your neighbors having a wild party with loud music, they'll come for that. They won't come out for this. They don't want to touch this."

Water Regulation

Jurisdiction and control over physical water resources (but not over water pollution, which is covered by the TCEQ) is distributed among "more than three dozen river authorities and special law districts, multiple aquifer authorities, nearly one hundred Groundwater Conservation Districts, sixteen Groundwater Management Areas, myriad water utilities, municipalities, and counties" (Rahm 2011, 2979). These are all in addition to the state agency, the Texas Water Development Board. These agencies, however, have exceedingly little ability to regulate actual water use (Yardley 2001).

In Texas no one "owns" the groundwater. If a person can drill a well into an aquifer, he or she can pump water out of it. "In Texas, all surface water is considered public, while groundwater is private. Under the 'rule of capture,' in Texas, a landowner can pump without regard for his neighbors. This can create a race to pump water before the aquifer goes dry, particularly with so much demand for it." (ibid.)

One activist called her local groundwater conservation district to complain about how much water the natural gas industry was using. "I'm concerned with the amount of water that I'm finding out online that [fracking] requires," she said. "They told me I *should* be concerned." And that was the extent of the response. The conservation district agreed that the amount of water used by the industry was a problem, but no concerted effort is being taken on the part of the conservation districts to change it.

Some small rural communities in the Shale have run out of water, or have seen water levels dip dangerously low.

Structural Constraints

Across agencies, I found that health-related investigations were prompted by citizens' complaints rather than being generated by the agency itself. Regular inspection of all of the more than 15,000 oil and gas sites in the Barnett Shale is difficult because the agencies' resources are limited.

"There's real constraints that we all work in no matter how much we want to do," one regulatory official told me. "Setting up an inspection report protocol that said we're going to cover our curfew hours [7 a.m. to 7 p.m., the period to which gas operations were restricted in that jurisdiction]. That's pretty easy to set up. Now what happens if we have an overnight incident? If we have an overnight incident that requires people to be out there, there are budget hits to that. Now some guy's on sixteen hours of overtime for the week, well deserved, definitely needs to get paid for, but that's coming out of the city's budget."

In addition to budgetary constraints, there are political ones. One activist spoke about her concern that a well was being drilled within 1,000 feet of her daughter's elementary school:

I've called the school. I've talked to the principal, and she refused to go to the city council meeting. She said "I can't go. If I go I will lose my job. I'll get fired. It's political." I said "No. This is health and safety. Don't you care? It's about the kids and it's, yeah it's political, but it's also a huge environmental and safety, health and safety issue." It's the politics of [the school district] and the teachers, principals, really can't have a say. Which seems wrong, doesn't it?

One thing that I found puzzling was the lack of data about how many active wells there were in a given city. Often officials had an estimate but did not know the actual number, and in some cases they didn't even know the locations of the equipment. In awareness of this problem, the TCEQ conducted a large inventory to map all the sites.

Another activist said this:

Once when they were done drilling and they had installed the well heads and the condensate tanks, it rained, and out there by the well heads there was this red fluid coming up out of the ground, and bubbles, constant bubbles. [We] filed a complaint with the Railroad Commission, and [the investigator] came out and said in his investigation report, said he couldn't find it. [We] filed another complaint. He came out, said he couldn't find it. Filed another complaint, he came out, and I was outside, and he's out there wandering around like he can't find it. Finally, I went out there and said "Right there." And the guy looked at it and I said "You ever seen that before?" "Nope." "Do you know what that is?" "Nope." "What are you going to test for?" "Chlorides." That's all they test for, chlorides.

The activists say that governmental agencies have failed them. They feel duped by the industry. While they attempt to gain some control through their activism, feelings of powerlessness dominate.

Gunter and Kroll-Smith (2007, 72–73) discuss the sense of betrayal that citizens feel when the government fails to adequately respond to environmental controversy into three categories: premeditated, structural, and equivocal.

The most insidious betrayals occur when governmental agencies intentionally try to deceive the public, acting in the interests of the industry, making deals behind closed doors, profiting at the community's expense, and covering up the industry's actions.

Structural betrayals occur when the residents assume that help will come from the agency but help is not forthcoming because of the agency's limitations. What the public may perceive as failures on the part of the agencies occur less because of any malfeasance on the part of the regulators than because of the bureaucratic nature of the organizations themselves. Weber (1930 [1958]) referred to the logic of bureaucracies as an "iron cage," meaning that bureaucracies operate fine on a normal day-to-day basis but are unable to function in emergencies. Perhaps they do not have the resources, the funding, or the legal authority to act. It is not that people within these agencies do not want to help, but rather that the structural constraints of their bureaucratic structure inhibits their response. These are the types of betrayals I witnessed most often in the Barnett Shale. The public's expectations of what the agency should be doing were often not in line with what the agencies were capable of doing.

The third type of betrayal that Gunter and Kroll-Smith (2007) identify is what they term "equivocal betrayal." In these cases, the intentions of the regulators are unclear. Did they operate in a "craven, reckless, and self-serving manner" (ibid., 72), or were their actions benign and only interpreted as miscreant by the citizens? It is uncertain. Conflicts arise when citizens and regulatory officials are "each viewing the conflict in a particular way, ignorant of the concerns and constraints facing the other party" and "local residents misinterpret the motives underlying agency actions, while agencies pursue policies which unintentionally harm local residents" (ibid., 94). In the Barnett Shale, conflicts and misunderstandings between regulators and residents are common and ongoing.

"There's nothing to stop them. No one will stop them," one activist lamented. Another mentioned that it felt like old-fashioned schoolyard bullying. "You have to do a lot of your own testing," she said, "especially if it's something that the Railroad Commission is responsible for testing. Unless you want to trust the operator—when the Railroad Commission requires testing, it's the operator that performs the testing. They take their own samples, or they hire their own labs. That's standard operating procedure."

Fragmentation and Confusion

Frustration with Texas' fragmented system resonates again and again in the interviews and the fieldwork. "I made some phone calls to our local health department," one activist said, "and they would pass the buck and give me a [phone] number [to someone else], and they would give me a number, and they would give me a number, and finally I gave up. There's like . . . It seems like there's no official place."

"They don't give a damn about health," another activist said, expressing his frustration with city officials. "They know about it and they hide it." From my vantage point throughout this project, I believe that the issue is not that regulatory officials don't care—I found many who do—but that they are severely limited in their abilities to respond to complaints. The piecemeal approach to regulation results in confusion over authority, diminished capacity to act, and distrust of the government.

One respondent told me a story about a farmer who had been concerned about naturally occurring radioactive material (NORM) from natural gas activities on his property and who claimed to have found a white powdery substance that was indicative of this sort of contamination: "He asked the Railroad Commission to come bring their Geiger counter to test it. They [the Railroad Commission] told him they lost their Geiger counter. They can't find it."

The Railroad Commission regulates the disposal of NORM; however, related health concerns (including issues such as recycling, decontamination, and movement of NORM) are regulated by the Texas Department of State Health Services. This fragmentation of authority is difficult to navigate, and I found instances within the regulatory agencies themselves when an employee did not know which agency was responsible for various aspects of regulation.

These agencies are bureaucracies, and bureaucracies excel at routinization. Procedures for operations are well established and are carried out in the same manner for each client. Because of their very structure, however, bureaucracies do not adapt quickly to change. "All too often," Gunter and Kroll-Smith write (2007, 88), "communities are caught in the gap between existing procedures and emergent needs. What this is likely to look like from the vantage point of the residents is that no government entity is making any apparent effort to protect them from harm." The idea that an agency has lost its Geiger counter seems absurd from the perspective of the community member who needs it. From the agency's point of view, though, it is likely that there are seldom (if, for all intents and purposes, ever) any calls for use of the equipment. The duty is outside of usual operations, perhaps spelled out in a dusty operations manual or in an obscure policy. The equipment, likely to have been purchased to fulfill the policy, was probably put on a shelf and forgotten. Though this does not in any way excuse the agency, it explains the situation.

In another case, an activist told me of trying to get remediation on a problematic waste pit near her home and encountering fragmented authority. She said that the pit stank of raw sewage:

They had actually taken the sewage from the tanks where they hook up to their mobile homes. They dumped the sewage into the pit. So I thought, ok, I've got them. Because drilling waste is not considered hazardous. There wasn't anything I could do about this horrible pit. But you cannot dump your sewage anywhere, so I thought, all right, I've got them. The first thing I called was the EPA. The guy was just appalled but he said if it's not in a water, a flowing water, we can't do anything about it. So you need to call the Railroad Commission. I was like, Oh God. But first I called some people I know who worked, used to work, in industry. Yeah. They do it all the time. That was just a typical thing for them to do. They do it all the time.

I called [the Railroad Commission] and they sent an inspector out there. He sent me an email and said "No, they didn't dump their sewage there." And I said "Yes they did." Now this stuff had been sitting in a tank in August for three months while they were drilling and they dumped it in there. I have this email [from the Railroad Commission that says] "The inspector did not find any toilet paper. So that means it can't be sewage."

The activist claimed that no samples were ever taken to test for sewage. She next called the local water board and her county commissioner. Both agencies said they could not help her. Tellingly, throughout her ordeal, no one had told her to contact her local health department—the one agency with the authority to do something about the dumping of sewage. She did not even realize she should have called the health department until I mentioned it after hearing her story.

Another activist shared her impressions of state agencies and expressed her frustrations in dealing with a multitude of responders:

People don't know what to do. They just keep getting the runaround so I try to help them through the process. The first few times they call one of the regulatory agencies it is so discouraging. The Railroad Commission is just condescending and hostile, so blatantly on industry's side that they pretty much give up after a time or two, they just give up. I have to keep telling them "No, you have to keep calling them." You have to keep calling them. We have to have the documentation. We have to show what an epic failure they are.

It's the same with the TCEQ, although you can sometimes get an individual investigator who's very caring and who wants to make a difference. They don't stay with the TCEQ. Their turnover is unbelievable. It is unbelievable! It seems like they promote failure. The people who are the weakest link get promoted and the others just disappear. We don't see them anymore. The ones who really want to do a good investigation and care and will do things like admit "Yeah, I smell that and I've got a sore throat. It's affecting me too." So they will want to do testing. They don't stay. They disappear.

You have this constant stream of new people coming in and they don't even know what they regulate. They don't know anything about it. Several weeks ago we had these storms—there's something that happens. When you have a storm, stuff happens at gas well sites. We don't know exactly what. If there's a power shutoff, then the pipeline power shuts off. But the gas well keeps producing. So it builds up pressure and it pops a valve and it releases. It sounds like a jet engine going off. I have a whole bunch of recorded 911 calls from Arlington where people are calling in, and you know, they are having health effects and they're calling 911. In one case the 911 operator told them "Well, it's just air and you don't need to be concerned." Yeah. It's just air. But I wouldn't light any matches.

Over time, the activists came to distrust the regulatory officials at all agencies. They claim that the regulatory agencies are all embedded with the industry. This outlook is likely a result of the fragmentation of authority and response. "We have to document everything," another activist said. "They're probably sick of us, but everything that's happened on our property—every spill, every leak, every odor—we've had to report. Yet nothing happens." The activists believe if they are able to document enough, they will be able to "prove" their case, they will be believed, and someone will finally do something.

On the other hand, one regulatory official discussed conflicts between himself and people who complain about the wells, signaling frustrations that even the regulatory officials feel:

People say "You need to come out here and test this." OK. Test what? There's all kinds of potential contaminants that could come off a site. Are you talking about air, water, soil, or all of them? The degree to which the media moves around is going to dictate how complicated it is to sample that. It is very difficult to get a good air quality sample off of these sites. It's very expensive in terms of being able to actually quantify contaminants. You can go out with a particular type of IR [infrared] camera and you can see emissions through that camera and that kind of stuff, but to actually go out . . . . People will say "We want to test for any kind of air quality contaminant." OK, well, you're probably talking about SUMA samplers, which are those pressurized samplers. They're essentially a container and they're cleaned at the laboratory so that all contamination is removed and then you have a vacuum. Then you set the orifice opening on that so that you have a particular amount of time that that thing is going to pull air in. That is deployed out in the field and it can do everything from collecting the entire volume over a minute or 24 hours depending on how you set it. But even that isn't as straightforward as it might seem. All right? Benzene, you've got benzene sources from gasoline stations, car exhaust, highways, you've even got some that's naturally occurring. So how do you separate out and say that a gas well is producing this benzene? Well, to do that you have to understand which direction the wind happens to be blowing. You need to cross your fingers that it's going to continue doing that during your entire sampling. You need to deploy some upwind. If you do that correctly you can get a sense for what's going on at the site, but you're talking, realistically, to do it right you need at least four canisters, and probably more than that. That's four deployments, four SUMA samplers, and four analyses that need to be done. That's extremely expensive. Trying to do that on a response basis to complaint is pretty difficult.

Now we will certainly go out there and visually inspect if there are noticeable odors or things of that nature, it can be pursued. If there's a concern about noise we can go out there and we've got devices that can tell us whether they're exceeding the noise requirements. If there's an obvious release of liquid then we know there's a problem there and we can deal with that. The air quality issue is tough, and that's what everybody seems to be concerned about.

We'd have to explain to everybody "Well, sample what?" "Air quality, just like I told you." Well, it isn't that easy. Are you talking about benzene and carbon disulfides? Those are some of the contaminants that people are really concerned about. Then [we] talk about what it would take to do the sampling effort, how [we] try to separate out from background and everyone realizes it's a much bigger issue . . . . It's not realistic I think to go out and expect to spend several days' worth of sampling and probably $20,000 worth of analytic on a complaint call. We'll get rid of our entire budget very quickly that way and we won't have any budget to do any more work.

Repeatedly, the activists told me that they contacted regulatory agencies so that their complaints about problems at specific sites would be documented—however, they said little to no follow-through happened. One man spoke about a company operating on his property with multiple documented violations—a company known for cutting corners: "[The company] admitted that the site was out of compliance for over a year. You feel like you're failed by your state agencies . . . . After a while you feel completely failed. And you know you are completely on your own."

When enforcement of violations does occur, the fines are negligible in comparison with the profits. One city official told me that, although the city can issue citations and penalties, the average penalty was $500 for a Class C misdemeanor, and up to $2,000 for health and safety misdemeanors. Fines levied by the U.S. Environmental Protection Agency can range into the tens of thousands of dollars, but these are rare. Many of the activists argue that the small fines do nothing to curb violations.

That there is a long lag between identification of an environmental health problem and remediation is well documented. Often years or even decades pass before remediation is complete, if it ever is. Brown (2007) notes that there is a similar pattern across cases of environmental contamination: Chemicals are treated as if they were harmless. Citizens' groups form and begin recording patterns of illness and other harms. They request governmental intervention. Eventually a regulatory agency may conduct an investigation. In nearly every case, the agency will determine that more time is needed to establish proof of harm. Meanwhile, locals continue to document their concerns (if they haven't given up—many do). Eventually, if the locals are very, very lucky, the agency might determine that remediation is necessary. This does not happen in most cases. Sometimes change is forced when private citizens sue the companies directly (an expensive and time-consuming approach that may fail). Often, change never comes.

Gunter and Kroll-Smith (2007, 70) review "the downward spiral of disintegrating relations between residents and officials" that happens in environmental controversies. "Government, it seems, often fails to respond to local environmental controversies and catastrophes in the manner citizens expect," they write. When this happens, distrust builds. The residents may perceive the response of the agencies as scattered or disorganized. They may view the regulators as hostile adversaries, or believe that officials simply don't care about their plight. They may also perceive that the regulatory officials are somehow in league with the industry, cutting back-room deals and, behind the scenes, profiting from the industry's activities.

One activist pointed out an interesting phenomenon that sums up her experiences. She talked about the maps used by both the industry and the regulators. I have seen many of the maps she talked about. "They don't put the houses on the maps," she said. "Cause it doesn't matter. We are not here. We do not exist."

A Tale of Three Cities

Within the Barnett Shale, the strategies activists employ differ from place to place. In this section, I discuss different approaches that citizens in three Barnett Shale cities have taken in their attempts to cope with natural gas activities. In each case, citizens felt compelled to do something about the drilling. For many of them—people spurred by their concern about possible health and safety implications of natural gas development in their cities—this involved kinds of political engagement that they had not previously experienced. In order to protect the privacy of informants, I have use fictional names for their cities. I have included comparable although not exact demographic data to portray a sense of place without detail that would enable a reader to pinpoint a setting or an informant.

In these particular cities, resident activists took three different approaches to protecting the health and safety of their communities: engagement in participatory democracy, changing the political players to induce more favorable legislation, and circumventing the politicians. As I will show, each of these approaches made inroads toward change. Although the results are quite different from jurisdiction to jurisdiction, ultimately citizen activists had a significant effect.

Oak Hollow

Activists in the city of Oak Hollow chose to work within the system, engaging in participatory democracy in order to make changes in their city oil and gas ordinance. Oak Hollow was one of the first cities in the Shale to enact an ordinance specific to gas drilling. That happened in the early 2000s. At that time, drilling was fairly new to the urban areas; however, city officials anticipated that there would be significant interest in drilling in the region and sought to act preemptively. After the ordinance was passed, the city hired an oil and gas coordinator to oversee a variety of matters related to natural gas, including legal issues, insurance requirements, leasing of city-owned property, site inspection, and permit reviews. Organizationally, this position was under the purview of the city's fire department.

A high percentage of adult residents of Oak Hollow hold college degrees. The average household income is about $55,000. One quadrant of the city is a light industrial area in which manufacturing and chemical processing take place. The city has a history of conflicts over polluting industry and environmental activism. There are multiple long-standing environmental organizations in the city, and they have been involved in multiple environmental controversies.

Concern over happenings in Dish (mentioned in chapter 3) and air-quality testing in other nearby towns prompted Oak Hollow officials to conduct their own study of whether gas sites in their city were contaminating surface water. They did not find evidence of such contamination.

Citizens protested a proposed natural gas well site that was adjacent to a neighborhood, an elementary school, and a nursing home. They argued that the placement of the well was too close to too many vulnerable people. They held protests at the site itself, wrote letters that were published in the local newspaper, and spoke about their concerns at city council meetings. Despite their protests, the well was constructed; however, their actions prompted the city council to revisit the oil and gas ordinance.

The city created an official task force made up of citizens to provide guidance to the city council as to what changes should be made in their oil and gas ordinance. Members of the city council appointed seven people to serve on the task force. The appointees included a spokesperson for the natural gas industry and an independent environmental consultant. The city council's goal was to solicit public input and to create a report detailing citizens' concerns for the city to consider.

The composition of the task force was challenged by local newspaper when reporters discovered that most of the members of the task force were not residents of the city. Despite repeated criticism, however, the membership was not changed. The newspaper also revealed significant financial ties between some of the members of the city council and the natural gas industry. One councilman, it reported, stood to earn a lot of money by leasing his mineral rights.

The city council issued a moratorium on new permits for the drilling and the production of natural gas until the process of revising the applicable ordinance was completed. One purpose of the moratorium was to stop a rush of applications for new wells in the hopes that they would be approved under less stringent rules (something that had happened in other cities); another was to give the city time to review some of the scientific and legal issues surrounding natural gas development. Many residents also hoped the moratorium would delay activities long enough so that stringent public-health protections could be put in place.

"Sitting on" drilling permits is a common practice. That is, companies often apply for and receive permits to drill, then allow some time to pass before any work is done. "Sitting on" a permit locks in the regulations that applied at the time the permit was given, and protects the company from changes that a city might make in its oil and gas ordinances.

While they debated changes to the ordinance, Oak Hollow officials repeatedly emphasized their desire for public input and their support for openness and dialogue among all parties with interests in the revised regulations. Minutes from meetings of the task force and support materials, such as power point presentations and white papers written by several groups, were posted on a dedicated website. City personnel continually expressed an ethic of transparency and a desire for democratic participation, although their actions were not always interpreted by the activists as consistent with those expressions.

While the official task force met, a group of activists formed a "shadow" group called Oak Hollow Citizens for Responsible Drilling (abbreviated OHCRD, which unfortunately came to be pronounced "Oh crud" and thus may have damaged the group's credibility). OHCRD had a pro-safety agenda and sought to advise the official task force on how to make Oak Hollow's oil and gas ordinance much stronger. OHCRD began as a platform for diverse voices and viewpoints in the drilling debate, initially representing both pro-safety and pro-drilling interests. Its meetings were open to the public and featured a number of by-invitation-only speakers. One meeting's panel discussion featured the mayor of a city that had already dealt with significant drilling issues; he shared the lessons he's learned. Another meeting featured an activist from a neighboring city who had been instrumental in the drafting of that city's oil and gas ordinance and a petroleum engineer with expertise in Barnett Shale activities. Many of the members of the city's official task force attended the OHCRD's meetings.

Eventually OHCRD dropped any pro-drilling pretense and became a voice for precaution and for stricter regulation. Its members increasingly saw the official task force as pro-industry and found themselves in conflict with the task force. "We became successful in becoming the voice of the citizens," one OHCRD activist told me. "Our foil is the official task force. They are the industry other. They're interested in subverting, somehow, the policy process." OHCRD members felt that, although the task force would humor their input, little of what they asked for would be in the final ordinance.

And that is exactly how it turned out. Despite their activities, OHCRD members were disappointed when the city released a draft of an ordinance for public comment. Most of the suggestions from OHCRD were not included.

Many OHCRD activists felt the actions of the city were, ultimately, a "dog and pony show," giving the impression of democracy without corresponding results. They continue to fight for better protections in Oak Hollow.

Finch

While activists in Oak Hollow worked within the political system to address their concerns about urban natural gas development, activists in the city of Finch worked to change the parameters of the system. They did this by changing the composition of the city's leadership, bringing in leaders with a pro-safety agenda.

Activism in Finch began in earnest when the local newspaper reported that a large compression facility, similar to the one in Dish, was going to be erected in Finch. That report prompted public action and mobilization in protest. Many residents objected to any industrial activity in the city.

Finch is a very affluent suburb on the Barnett Shale, with a median household income of $130,000, and its citizens are highly educated. It is very difficult to find any evidence of poverty in the city. There is also a high level of civic engagement—indeed, such engagement is considered a status symbol. Organizations such as the Junior League and the League of Women Voters have high profiles and are involved in civic projects. The local political scene in Finch is a study in contentious politics, complete with factions and ongoing drama.

Generally speaking, the residents are politically conservative. Finch is primarily a bedroom community; that is, most residents commute to nearby cities. There are few businesses (mostly upscale restaurants and grocery stores), and aside from natural gas extraction there is no industry to speak of. The city is filled with beautifully manicured green spaces, including parks and "natural" areas. Most of the city is quite lovely. The majority of homes might be referred to as "McMansions." The schools are known for their high quality and have been designated as exemplary by the Texas Education Agency. The roads and public spaces are well maintained. Driving through the city, a person might be hard pressed to believe that the rest of the country has been experiencing an economic recession.

Finch is not the sort of place one would expect to be an environmental sacrifice zone. Nor would one expect residents to feel disenfranchised. These are people with education, money, and social capital.

The first gas well in the city (known to locals as the Quin Site) was drilled in 2004. Seventy-six wells had been drilled in the city by the fall of 2012, many of them in those lovely green spaces, and many more sites had received permits for drilling.

The Quin Site became a focus of concern because of its proximity to a public elementary school. The school and a large residential neighborhood sit downwind from the site. The distance between the edge of the Quin pad and the perimeter of the elementary school building is less than 1,000 feet, and the pad is within 500 feet of the school's athletic fields.

Through a process of public epidemiology, activists identified problems with the Quin Site, documented in both Texas Railroad Commission and the Texas Commission on Environmental Quality records. This site was flared often in its early stages, which suggested a need to burn off toxic chemicals. Monitoring of ambient air quality near the site found levels of carbon disulfide and benzene higher than those considered acceptable for long-term exposure. An investigation by the Railroad Commission found that the cement casing on the well had not hardened properly and had cracked. The public epidemiologists also identified what they believed to be high levels of thyroid cancer, breast cancer, and childhood leukemia in the adjacent neighborhood.

Many residents were outraged when they learned that a compression station was going to be built in their town and wanted the city council to keep it out. Frustrated with the council's pro-drilling stance, they formed an organization called Finch Neighbors United. FNU prepared a so-called petition ordinance that specified the changes it wanted to see in the city's oil and gas ordinance. Should at least 15 percent of the city's registered voters sign a petition ordinance, the city council is required to either accept the ordinance as written or else put it on the next ballot for a public vote. FNU collected over 6,000 signatures, more than enough for the citizens and the council to consider the petition a mandate for change.

As has already been noted, the political scene in Finch is contentious. The debate over the compression station took place as an election was approaching and thus served as an ideal opportunity to replace some of the members of the city council. More than half of the members of the council were voted out of office in that election and replaced with people who professed to favor safe drilling. The new city council adopted some of the provisions that had been demanded in the petition ordinance, but not all of them. Not all of the FNU's members were happy with the results. Some felt that natural gas drilling had been used as a platform to get people elected to office but hadn't produced the follow-through that they wanted. Others felt betrayed when the new city council failed to strengthen the oil and gas ordinance to their satisfaction. In the midst of the political turmoil, some of the oil and gas companies used the discord to their advantage, "slipping in permits" before the ordinance became more stringent.

Ultimately the city of Finch drafted an ordinance that came to be hailed as among the most protective in the Barnett Shale. However, the process was so contentious that it split the supporting voting base, and many of the activists who were involved still express dissatisfaction with the outcome.

Ironton

Citizens' responses in the city of Ironton looked different from activities in Oak Hollow and Finch. Rather than working with the city council or dismantling it to protect health and safety, some of the residents circumvented the city's authority by negotiating directly with the gas industry.

Ironton is a suburb of Fort Worth with a population of about 50,000. The residents are largely working-class and middle-class. The average household income is $48,000. Unusual in Texas, homeowners in the city's large Larkspur neighborhood owned a percentage of their mineral rights. Larkspur is an older neighborhood, with homes built in the 1930s and the 1940s—long before there was any interest in natural gas development in this part of Texas.

As often happens when gas exploration begins in an area, one of the natural gas companies interested in drilling in the neighborhood leafleted Larkspur with fliers touting the benefits of the natural gas industry. The company offered to lease mineral rights from residents who owned all or part of them.

"So many people were signing up just like that," one of the activists involved told me, snapping his fingers. "It's free money. Five hundred bucks for my house, or you know, if I own half the mineral rights it's two-fifty or whatever. Free money! Without even thinking about it."

But an initially small group of homeowners did start thinking about it. They decided to host a neighborhood meeting, after which they leafleted the area with fliers of their own saying: "Gas drilling is coming to the area. You might not want it. Come find out more." About two hundred people from the neighborhood came to the meeting.

"If you put political fliers on people's doors," one of the activists from Ironton told me, "you can walk all damn day long and maybe get one response. But this stuff involved money and property and people turned out in force."

After the initial meeting, several small groups of people concerned about the drilling were formed. They organized over the Internet, launching Yahoo and Facebook groups. A seasoned social activist in the neighborhood contacted each of these groups, and they pulled together to strategize collectively and formed a formal nonprofit organization, the Larkspur Neighborhood Association. After electing of board of directors, they drafted a memorandum of understanding between individual homeowners and the association and presented it to people in the neighborhood. "By signing this," one member of the association told me, "it didn't commit them to anything. It just says 'I'm on your team.' So we gathered up, we had over the course of a year, 700 of those from different families." The association's board of directors reviewed mineral lease contract proposals from the gas companies for all of the families and assisted the families through the process. There wasn't always a clear consensus about what should be done. One activist said:

Everybody wanted clean air and water. Not everybody believed that drilling would affect that, but most people were willing to say "OK, let's put that in the contract." If they say it's clean, put it in writing. We pretty much decided that if we got together, if we fought each other, if we had a pro-drilling group and an anti drilling group, then neither of us would win. The anti-drilling group would get ripped off because they would get crappy money for their rights. The anti-drilling group would lose. The pro-drilling group would lose. Everybody would just get a dirty well and low money.

The more we looked at it as a Board, and studying it, the more we came to the conclusion: This is pretty bad. Or it could be pretty bad. But we didn't think there was a chance in hell of stopping it.

Their collective action gave the neighbors some power relative to the industry that none of them would have held in isolation. There was prime shale beneath their homes, and their holding at least some of the mineral rights meant that they could bargain. Negotiating collectively ensured that both majority and minority concerns were addressed.

The Larkspur Neighborhood Association wrote into the contracts that the gas company would carry a large insurance policy in case of explosion or other disaster, such that all homeowners would be covered. They included mandatory water testing of surface water within a certain radius of a proposed pad site at least sixty days before the beginning of any activity to ensure they had baseline water-quality data. If future concerns over water quality arose, the association could more readily seek remedial action from the gas company. The company argued against some of the association's proposals, but the collective action empowered the homeowners and eventually their demands were met.

The association also created a website that provided updates on natural gas drilling in the city. It featured an interactive map showing the locations of homes, schools, parks, and gas wells, information on the ownership of the wells, and links to the websites of city and state regulators and those of the natural gas companies operating in the neighborhoods.

As part of the final contract with the gas company, the company donated $75,000 to the association. This money was used to conduct baseline air-quality studies in the neighborhood and continued air monitoring as needed. Should the monitoring signal a change in air quality, the organization could then address the issue with the company. The organization also completed other projects with the funds, including building a playground and a community garden in the neighborhood.

Residents of Larkspur were also protected by Ironton's oil and gas ordinance, but that ordinance is quite weak relative to those of other cities in the Shale. Working in partnership with the industry, citizens circumvented the city council, creating their own agreements with the industry and writing their desired protections into their mineral leasing contracts. The homeowners had the power to do this only because of a willingness of people in the neighborhood to join together and because— even more important—they owned at least a partial claim to the mineral rights.

Ordinance as Talisman

Activists in the three cities mentioned above seem to have focused most of their attention on city oil and gas ordinances. The residents tended to think the cities had a much greater legal ability to regulate than they actually had. Because the state-level regulations were so lenient, city ordinances were the only means by which some control over the industry's practices could be maintained (although, as was noted earlier, cities' powers in regard to oil and gas regulation are weak in Texas). This scenario fits into a larger culture in Texas over state-versus-city clashes of authority. While many politicians at the state level argue for limited federal intervention (and for states' rights), these same people fight against allowing the city governments too much autonomy.

Strong oil and gas ordinances became the talismans of this fight. Activists believed that such ordinances could protect people from the industry. The document was imbued with magical-like properties of security, the one hope citizens held for protection from the industry.

While the ordinances addressed a variety of aspects related to urban natural gas development, perhaps the most visible and contested issue within the ordinances had to do with setbacks. A setback is the distance between a gas well and a Protected Use property. (Most Protected Use properties are homes, but cities also could designate other sites, such as churches, schools, or hospitals.) The greater the distance between a natural gas well and a Protected Use property, the greater the sense of safety in the community.

One activist spoke of trying to convince his city council to change the city's ordinance to expand the setbacks from 500 feet to 1,000 feet: "It's 500 feet from the center of the bore to the edge of the dwelling. So for instance, if your house was here and you had 100 feet of yard, they're using up your 100 feet. You could put the center of the well [500 feet away from the edge of the house], but then you could put tanks and stuff 100 feet from a person's house. Not 100 feet from their property. From their house." Requiring a bigger setback, the activist argued, would mean less exposure to toxic chemicals for the people residing nearby. Research into chemical exposures near natural gas sites supports this notion; as was noted in chapter 3, studies have found that the risk of health effects from drilling-associated chemicals increases the closer people reside to the pads.

Across the cities of the Barnett Shale, oil and gas ordinances became focal points for activists. Unfortunately, changes to local ordinances have no effect on wells already drilled and permitted—those fall under the previous rules. Every detail—every word—of the ordinances was fought over, although in most cases the end result was less stringent than the activists had hoped.

As each city crafted its own ordinance, there was variation between how restrictive the cities were. As a result, protections differed from place to place, and the industry was "pushed" into areas with less restrictive ordinances.

5   Reluctant Activists

Jeremy and I sit at a picnic table across the street from a gas drilling operation. We are eating snow cones at a small stand that has opened up for the summer. He pauses as an eighteen-wheel tanker truck turns in to the site, then tells me a story:

A guy called me one day—I think it was 2007, summer 2007; it can't be that long ago, can it? 2008 maybe—[and] said "Hey we got a notice in our door that somebody wants to lease our mineral rights." This is not too far from my house, and I was like "Well that's crazy, I didn't think that [drilling activity] was over this far [east]."

He stops talking and takes a few bites of his snow cone. His is blue. Mine is red, strawberry. I hold it against my temple to try to cool off. It is over 102 degrees outside. There is a loud clanging sound, coupled with the sounds of multiple running engines, coming from across the street, and the air is thick with diesel exhaust. Jeremy chose this location for his interview to make a point about just how bad urban drilling is. He's made it.

I went over and talked to the guy and I saw his paper. He made a copy of it, and you know, they were offering, what was it, $2,500 an acre at 20 percent, and it was right here in the neighborhood. They didn't say where the drill site was going to be. . . . It was alarming. I hadn't really looked into nearly the depth of it until that happened. . . . I went and I sat with him and I looked into it, and then I started staying up late at night and just reading everything I could read about the Barnett Shale and how the process works and what can go wrong, and if you ever get on YouTube and start looking at videos of all the stuff that could go wrong . . . .

He shrugged his shoulders, sighed, and continued:

I mean, you just watch video after video after video stuff blowing up and leaking and spilling.

According to Spiegel (2009), "public health literature has taken an increasing interest in the concept of environmental justice, often understood as the unequal spatial distribution of pollution and toxicity and the disproportionate environmental burden borne by racial minorities and poorer communities." As I embarked on this project, knowing the literature on environmental justice, I expected to find natural gas wells in lower socioeconomic neighborhoods. Instead I found myself conducting interviews in $250,000–$500,000 homes. How could these people, with so much privilege, be suffering from environmental injustice? I was continually confronted with a notion that I am calling the reluctant activist. The people in my study were primarily white, middle-class to upper-middle-class, and highly educated, and they possessed social capital. They did not identify with oppressed minority groups. Before the arrival of natural gas drilling in their communities, social activism was not part of their identity. Politically conservative, they viewed protesting as something that only liberals and/or Democrats do. Once engaged in activism, they had a strong sense of altruism. They identified "professional" and "hero" activists, and did not want to be seen as either. Despite their social capital, they also encountered barriers to political participation, and found themselves impotent in the shadow of the oil and gas industry.

Lerner (2012, 8) writes that "fence line residents experience a moment of rude awakening—an awful surprise—when they learn that they have been exposed to elevated levels of toxic chemicals." He notes that many members of the middle class have been sheltered from industrial sites and are not aware of how bad such sites can be.

The activists with whom I spoke had become involved in a variety of ways, but each of them had made a connection between natural gas drilling and threats to their health. They had "had their eyes opened" in some manner or another. Some had read news articles about the effects of toxic chemicals at the gas wells that sparked their concern. One said she had seen some protesters holding signs alongside the road. She approached them and asked what they were protesting, and they told her about gas drilling. "I felt like a sociologist," she said. "I'll just check it out. Before you know it, I'm holding a sign." Another activist told me:

I was just doing a random search on the Internet: gas drilling, hazards, dangers, or health effects or whatever. I don't even remember what I Googled, but I came across this article. I was so disturbed by what I saw. I don't even remember the content of the article, but it was somebody's life that was just devastated by drilling. Their animals died, and sickness, and environmental things, and water contamination . . . . The more I learned, the more horrible the story seemed.

Another woman told me about the rude awakening that had prompted her to become an activist:

My experience started with thumper trucks. I became totally aware of it. I kind of knew about this issue as it was coming up. But it hadn't directly impacted me until I turned the corner one morning going to work and there were these thumper trucks.

I'm not sure if you've ever seen a thumper truck. These are seismic testing trucks. They drop a one-thousand pound weight to the ground in front of wherever they decide to look for gas, natural gas. This is how they discover where the pockets, where the sweet spots they call them, are in the Barnett Shale. You would think that they would never have gone into where people are living house to house in a neighborhood. That it just would not have been done. Ever! And yet they just do it. They came in during the day, while people were at work and they didn't know [gas exploration] was going on during the day time in their neighborhoods.

They drop a 1,000-pound weight to the ground and shake the ground. They're basically creating a little bit of seismic activity. . . . They put there antennas throughout the area they're testing.

The day the thumpers came. A day that will live in infamy, that's what I like to call it. So I turned the corner and there are these three trucks. They're ushering, you know like when workmen will usher you [in traffic], and your tendency is just to follow what they tell you to do because there might be some reason why you should get out of the way. I started to get curious about it and tried to figure out what was going on. I pulled over and I stopped. And that's probably where my life changed. Seriously. Because if I had pulled away and gone . . . . So I'm pulling up and I stop my car. I get out. And there's one of my neighbors, this lady. She had come out of her home and she was hysterical pretty much. The lady that came out of her house, very conservative woman. I knew who she was. She said inside her home was just shaking. She was coming out of her home just really upset, right? And it was real loud right in front of her home cause that's where the trucks were, and she said "What are they doing?" She says to me "Are they drilling for gas? Are they drilling for oil?" She thought they were drilling. She had no clue. And there's this policeman that showed up, and he ushered me over, not her.

The policeman asked *me*, what are they doing, pointing at the thumper. He saw how upset the citizens were and he's supposed to be protecting the citizens. Then this guy comes over, with his hard hat on, he's got his clipboard and his hard hat.

What's that cognitive dissonance thing? You're just standing there going— there's something really weird about all this and I can't quite—she calmed down. The policeman was confused. The guy wanted my name and number. I got to go to work, right? I got in my car and left.

When I got to work I told my boss about it. She said there was a city council meeting that night and this was one of the things they were going to talk about. I said "I don't go to city council and complain," you know? But it was real upsetting to me. I felt like I needed to say something.

And she did. She has been an activist since that day.

Buying Safety

Szasz (2007) writes about the tendency of middle-class Americans to try to buy their way out of environmental harm rather than engaging in collective efforts to enact social change. People use their purchasing power to buy their way to safety, buying bottled water rather than organizing for better water quality, buying organic produce rather than insisting on a nationwide agricultural policy for organics, or buying natural body care products rather than insisting on federal oversight into product safety. Szasz refers to this tendency as an inverted quarantine, an individualized attempt of people to isolate themselves from environmental hazards.

Though residents in many areas of the natural gas fields of North Texas often have significant social capital relative to other sacrifice zones in the United States, their social capital is nothing in comparison with the resources of the oil and gas industry (particularly in Texas). Unless they are able to move out of the region, people living in proximity to natural gas operations cannot buy their way to safety. Residents who are afraid of harm from the industry's practices and who want to protect themselves and their families must either relocate or engage in political action. For many of the people I interviewed, this was a new experience. They did not have a history of political participation, and they entered into participation reluctantly.

In many cases, residents paid out of pocket, often in the amounts of tens of thousands of dollars, for independent testing of the air and/or the water for pollutants. I spoke with two activists, Alicia and Tracy, about this expensive attempt to buy safety. "They look at this as democratizing science," Alicia said. "But actually it's a sign of a breakdown. This should be the government's role. Why isn't the TCEQ out there testing?" "Yeah," Tracy added. "It's parents who are lucky enough to have enough money and are worried about their kids' health." "There's important justice issues here," Alicia said. "Really important ones, because our model of innovation is run with it once it's profitable and then monitor it for problems. Cobble solutions on the back end. That's what we're stuck doing, but who's doing the monitoring? Poor people who live next to that shit? That's the inequality."

"But the rich people have the money to do something about it," I added.

"Yeah, but they do have to monitor it. And they do have to be engaged and they still have to write their ordinances," Alicia said. "All of the onus of action and burden of proof is on . . . "

"The citizens," Tracy said, "instead of the industry."

Activism, monitoring, collecting data—these activities take significant amounts of time, money, and energy. Activists are unpaid volunteers who work on this issue of their own accord, in contrast to highly paid industry executives, public relations firms, and paid regulatory officials. It is the industry and regulators' jobs to participate in policy making and other activities; the activists must do all of their work in their spare time. They must educate themselves on highly technical matters. They must find time to go to meetings, and get someone to watch their children so they can participate. Keeping up with the issues alone is a challenge. Some of the activists also deal with active health problems that they believe are caused by the drilling. All this continues while life moves on. "I just need to get on with my life. I need to have a normal life where I can spend time with my family and live a normal life. You start getting sucked into this. It will consume every minute of the day. You don't get any money for doing it. I mean, I need money to pay my bills right now," one activist said.

Lerner (2012) identifies a typical pattern in environmental justice activism. First, residents experience a "rude awakening" upon discovering that they are being exposed to toxins. They appeal to regulatory officials, from whom they get the "runaround." They begin to conduct their own research into the problem, and in doing so they identify structures of racism at work in their exposure. Grassroots organization happens after a galvanizing event, such as a news report or an explosion. Grassroots organizers search for allies to help them with their fight. They collect documentation to demonstrate harm to others.

Popular Epidemiology

Brown (1992, 269) focuses on the data collection and documentation the grassroots participants engage in, calling this process "popular epidemiology." Through his research, Brown has identified a typical pattern to popular epidemiology. The process begins as residents identify clusters of illness and identify pollution-causing hazards separately, then connect the two into a causal relationship. They share information with one another, building a hypothesis of harm. They turn to regulatory officials and scientists for information, and they begin to organize. They convince regulatory agencies to conduct illness investigations, and in the majority of cases the agency finds no conclusive relationship. They then seek external assistance, finding other experts to conduct investigations. After gathering evidence, they confront the polluting company, often through litigation, and they seek official corroboration of the problem. Indeed, Gunter and Kroll-Smith (2007, 122) characterize "the emergence of citizen science to challenge the assertions of a corporate- or government-sponsored science" as "a key flashpoint in local environmental controversies."

Popular epidemiologists play an important part in activism related to drilling for natural gas. All of the reluctant activists I spoke with spent significant amounts of time collecting information about the health and environmental impacts of gas drilling and becoming lay experts on the various aspects of natural gas extraction. Popular epidemiologists draw on a variety of sources of knowledge, including peer-reviewed journal articles, government publications, and anecdotal data (Gullion, Henry, and Gullion 2008). They undertake a complex process to gather and interpret scientific data and knowledge resources in order to explain a health condition (Brown 1992; Davison et al. 1991). They also "[arm] themselves with the lingual resources of toxicology, environmental impact assessment, biomedicine, risk inventories, nuclear engineering, and other instruments of reason" (Gunter and Kroll-Smith 2007, 122).

"Hell, I didn't know anything!" an activist told me. "It's all discovery for me. I have a curious mind about all this. It kept me engaged, figuring it out."

Jennifer, a reluctant activists with whom I spent a lot of time, carries notebooks of data everywhere she goes. She can whip out a laminated table or chart and point out when toxins permeate the air around her home. She has poster-size maps detailing proximities of gas pads to homes and schools, complete with prevailing wind patterns to illustrate potential airborne chemical exposures. One map has tiny stars marking the homes of people who have been diagnosed with cancer. A tendency to wield reams of supporting data is common among the activists I studied. They create their own science and challenge the regulators, believing that if they can prove their case they will get the remedial assistance they seek.

Activism in the Face of Opposition

Cole and Foster (2001) identify three aspects of the lives of people who become environmental health activists and explore their motives, backgrounds, and perspectives. They write that environmental health activists work in their local community to promote health and safety. The activists fight for the protection of their own homes, their families, and their community. In most previous studies of environmental health activism, the activists are poor or working class, people of color, and are socially disenfranchised. They have a social justice orientation, and they often see their communities in general (whether racial or ethnic minorities or other minority groups) as being under attack by the dominant groups. Environmental problems are one more instance of racism. They are aware of structural inequities, and they view this as another facet of such inequities.

In contrast with Cole and Foster's work, the activists in my study did not have a social justice orientation before their experience in activism. The reluctant activists viewed protesting as something that liberals and Democrats—not they—do. Both environmental activism and protesting were framed by the reluctant activists as counter to conservative beliefs. The reluctant activists said they were often discredited as "liberal ideologues," and that the labels "liberal" and "Democrat" harmed their knowledge claims.

Most of the reluctant activists identified themselves as either Republicans or fiscal conservatives. This is in keeping with the demographics of the area. The population in the Barnett Shale region is predominantly conservative. Most voter precincts are "red" (i.e., favor Republicans), and Republicans hold a majority of elected offices.

One activist told me "They call us 'Commies,' and 'Obama lovers,' and all kinds of *crazy* stuff, because we are trying to protect the community, trying to protect the environment." In a snarky voice she said "Oh, that is the world of *liberal activists*," then laughed. "It's funny," she continued, "because this is a politically conservative area . . . . We're not hired guns. We are people who decided that in addition to carpool, we need to protect the neighborhood. The pro-drillers, they really try to take 'activists' and make it a dirty word. But every once in a while you get issues in your town that make it important enough to really get involved in politics."

Another activist talked about how his city council responded to his concerns about natural gas drilling in his neighborhood: "We weren't opposed to it. We *were not* opposed to it. All we wanted was for [the gas company] to have their emissions plan. 'Please table this' [we asked the city council]. Their plan is shit. They need to fix it. Well, you would have thought we just went up there waving the communist flag and said no gas drilling."

"You don't want to [be an activist], because the moment you do you're an environmental wacko, you're a liberal," another activist said. "But I know who I am. I've always been conscious of the environment. I'm also a conservative. We recycle. I'm still the same person I was before. If anything, what happened to us pushed us into becoming more active in this issue."

One activist told me a story about helping housewives become protesters in an affluent, largely conservative community in the Shale:

I have these pictures of the people [protesting]. I mean, these are soccer moms standing with a truck this close [she holds her hands inches apart] to their stomach where they would not let them pass. They have posters that say "Gas and greed divides communities." I made them these little paper cut-out gas masks and they put them on popsicle sticks and held them up [to their faces]. That's some activism that those people did and it was pretty amazing because these are soccer moms. They were afraid to do it, too. They were so afraid to do it. Some of them were really fierce and they stood there and the trucks were right there. They stood with their signs and they wouldn't move until the sheriff made them. The sheriff made them move and they moved. They stood to the side and protested. Then some of them were so nervous about it. They had their little matching tennis outfits on and their little golf carts and they were driving around. And they would scoot off to the side and then they would come back. It was great.

These people had never participated in a public protest before. Indeed, they said, as did many of the other activists, that standing on the side of a road with signs was not something they, as conservatives, would do. Doing so was not an expression of their usual politics until natural gas drilling became an issue in their neighborhoods—until they felt they *had* to do something about it.

Across the interviews, I heard the same refrain: "I never thought I would be doing this." The reluctant activist is a bit surprised to find himself or herself in this role. "You feel like you've just been thrust into this different universe," one activist told me. Another said "I just kind of fell into this political activism mostly because I wanted my family to be safe." Social activism was not a facet of the reluctant activist's identity before this.

Altruistic Activism

Once they transitioned into "this different universe," the reluctant activists formed an altruistic opinion about the nature of their activism. "You have people who think they are gonna be the next Erin Brockovich," one woman told me. "They're gonna be on TV and they wanna be the one who's quoted in the paper. You can't do this for that reason."

The activists often spoke of "Erin Brockovich wannabes." This was a derogatory comment directed at other activists. Activists of that sort, they felt, did not truly care about the issue as much as they wanted to be the darling or the hero of the movement. Many of the activists referred to one another in this manner. Anyone who was particularly engaged and vocal could acquire the label. Once a person had acquired it, he or she was treated as an outsider by the rest of the group. The entire time I was involved in this project, I never once heard a man referred to as "an Erin Brockovich." That designation was given, by both male and female activists, only to women. When a man was in the spotlight—even if he stumbled or preened—he seldom received any criticism from fellow activists. Male activists seemed to receive much more support from the community of activists than women received. There were also notably fewer men than women actively engaged, yet the women often deferred to the male activists—even when the women had been involved longer and were much more knowledgeable about the issues.

In the conversation I quoted at the beginning of this section, the woman expressed her dissatisfaction with other activists who spoke with newspaper and other reporters: "I see these [other activists] and I'm going 'You can't speak, and I'm sorry. This may be egotistical, but you can't speak to this issue like I can. I've been doing this a lot of years.'" Not surprisingly, this woman was labeled "an Erin Brockovich" by her peers. Passion and dedication were often viewed in a negative light when coupled with media attention. It was thus important for activists to be involved, to go to meetings and to speak out, but not to personally gain too much attention for themselves. Unfortunately, this created antagonism between the activists and seemed to fragment their power.

For the reluctant activists, activism has clear boundaries. They had a very clear picture of what an activist should be—and the center of attention was not it. They clearly felt that an activist should be altruistic and should work, without ego involvement, for the good of the community.

"The whole reason I'm doing this is not for myself," another woman said. "It's not to see my name in the paper. It's for my kids. It's for my family. It's for my community. That's why I'm doing it."

The people I studied felt protected by their social capital. As they believed that they had the power to prevent these things from happening, their sense of protection was violated by the industry and by the lack of governmental regulation. Theirs is not simply a matter of a privileged response. As Johnson and Sciccitano (2012) noted, "NIMBY" (standing for "not in my back yard") is typically a negative expression for people who want the conveniences that a hazardous facility may ultimately provide without being personally impacted by that facility (for example, wanting their garbage collected but not wanting to live near a garbage dump). Van der Horst (2007, 2705) notes that "although most researchers now seem to agree that this phenomenon is rather complex, and that the 'selfish' element is only one of the many possible reasons why many people may oppose a particular local development, the acronym [NIMBY] is still widely used in academia." The term was also widely used by the participants in my study. They recognized the term as negative and tried to distance themselves from it. Across my interactions with them, the activists emphasized that they wanted not only to protect their families and their local community but to protect *all* communities from the hazards associated with natural gas extraction. This was in keeping with the desire not to be "an Erin Brockovich."

We Americans want cheap electricity. We want the benefits afforded by natural gas, but we do not want the associated pollution. Nearly all of the reluctant activists were not opposed to natural gas per se (indeed, one interview took place in a kitchen with a large restaurant-style gas stove); rather, they wanted the drilling of gas wells and the extraction of gas to be safe. They were even agreeable to having limited natural gas activities in their communities. But they wanted the extraction to be done in a manner in which no one's health would be compromised. Many researched safer techniques, such as "green completions" rather than open flaring, and presented their ideas to city councils. Unfortunately, they seldom saw policy changes result from those efforts.

Reluctant activists often expressed mixed feelings about natural gas. Here is an example:

For our area, they've projected thirty years of drilling, I think, in the Barnett Shale. There might be different estimates. That's a huge growth opportunity. How can you deny that? How can you deny the beauty of getting energy from our own soil? I mean, there are a lot of advantages to it. Maybe on the surface, if I would've seen this without really knowing about the operation involved I would've been really excited about it. Because I am for getting energy from our land as much as we can. And keeping it at home. And the benefit the people are hopefully going to get in the area with jobs and whatever. But it seems like there are other things in the equation. Maybe you don't get the benefits. Or, what are the risks and benefits and how do they weigh out?

This activist became aware of the issue through media coverage that questioned the safety of gas drilling. Because she works in the health care industry, she said she saw red flags—things that raised her concern about the effects of natural gas development on public health. Like many other activists, she was not against urban gas development per se; rather, she wanted safeguards in place to ensure that "this whole production is the safest that it could be so that we don't have lasting environmental impacts." She continued: "People are claiming they're experiencing damaged health. I want to try to avoid, to work in whatever way I need to, to help those situations."

Repeatedly, the people I interacted with in the course of my study claimed that gas companies are not motivated by the need to protect the public's health. If anything, they argued, public health stands in the way of profit.

Social Privilege and Environmental Injustice

As Cole and Foster (2001) note, dozens of studies have borne out the notion that environmental hazards affect poor people and people of color disproportionately. Most of these studies focus on siting disputes. Siting disputes involve the physical placement of polluting facilities (such as municipal waste dumps, storage and incineration facilities for hazardous waste, or chemical refineries) near residences.

Residential areas in close proximity to environmental hazards, termed "sacrifice zones" by Lerner (2012), typically are populated by poor people and/or people of color. This environmental racism is the foundation of environmental justice theory, which posits that people in poverty, particularly people of color, are disproportionally affected by pollution and disproportionally exposed to toxic chemicals. Numerous studies demonstrate that race is highly correlated with exposure to hazardous chemicals and with unequal enforcement of environmental regulations.

The siting of oil and gas drilling, and of other mining operations, is based on geology. In the Barnett Shale, the ability to extract the minerals was developed after the growth of middle-class communities. Those communities were already in place, and were in the way of the minerals. This is very different from other siting conflicts, in which the siting is flexible and facilities are placed in impoverished areas. It also is very different from mining that takes place before urban growth.

Environmental justice as it is classically defined argues that one sector of society benefits from environmental harm in another sector. Sacrifice zones tend to be impoverished neighborhoods and neighborhoods with high numbers of minority residents; however, the literature on environmental justice and mining complicates this connection (Stretesky and Lynch 2011). This is particularly problematic in the Barnett Shale, where the population infrastructure was in place *before* the natural gas industry began to drill.

When one is considering environmental justice and mining, a purely quantitative approach may not be as useful as it is in other siting scenarios. Identification geographically of sites with pockets of racial and ethnic disparity—a typical and illuminating methodology of environmental justice scholars—makes less sense when one is considering mines. Mines are sited where minerals are present. Yet this does not mean that the burden of environmental impact is distributed equitably. Keeling and Sandlos (2009) call for a historical, narrative approach to uncovering environmental injustices in mining areas. They criticize the tendency of the environmental justice literature to focus on siting (that is, the locating of hazardous facilities, such as chemical plants or landfills, in neighborhoods of lower socioeconomic status). Environmental justice concerns itself with marginalized, racialized groups that are exposed to hazards that are beyond their control. However, Keeling and Sandlos write (2009, 118), "traditional environmental justice perspectives alone—with their emphasis on distributed injustice in waste siting decisions and the quantification of environmental inequity—are inadequate to comprehend the particular roots and dynamics of mining's unequal social and environmental legacies." "Mineral develop-ment," they continue, "is not easily reducible to a siting issue within an environmental justice framework. As any miner will tell you, mines are sited where viable ore deposits are found, not necessarily where pliant or disenfranchised communities are located."

Homeowners' wealth and socioeconomic status give them less power in mining cases than other environmental justice narratives. The minerals are where they are. If the industry wants to get underneath a particular home, it doesn't matter if that home cost $30,000 or $1 million; the industry will do everything it can to drill under it.

Figueroa (2006, 372) argues for a multi-dimensional definition of envi-ronmental justice—a definition that includes disenfranchisement from policy making and "discrimination against the groups' environmental identity." Urkidi and Walter (2011, 684) have called for broadening the scope of environmental justice to include "a wide range of power, gender, identity, cultural and institutional concerns." Urkidi and Walter also call for examination of structural factors, institutional factors, and political and social processes involved in justice debates.

Although the activists I studied have high levels of social capital, I often found the appearance of political engagement without correspond-ing political power. Real barriers exist to participating in the political process, such as access to child care so as to be able to attend evening meetings and domination of city-council-appointed committees by repre-sentatives of the gas industry. Such structural barriers to participation would fall under Figueroa's multi-dimensional configuration of environ-mental justice.

Constant vigilance takes its toll. "My biggest frustration," one activist told me, "is that this has taken 50 percent of my life"—'this' meaning "to observe, to safeguard the health and safety of my family." Another activist told me the following:

Every time you call, or you file a complaint online, you're giving up at least twelve hours of your life. You have to wait twelve hours, stay here and wait. There was one time [my spouse] complained, and it was in the evening, it was a compressor station that had lost power. It was about ten o'clock at night, and you could hear it outside. So he filed a complaint. They called him back after midnight, and we were all asleep. They put in their investigation report that they tried to call us and that they couldn't find the site, so they went on to something else. Even though the TCEQ has GPS coordinates of the site and the name of the site.

Accounts of the complainant having to guide the investigator through the complaint came up repeatedly in the interviews—stories of citizens taking hours out of their lives to walk investigators through their complaint, to go to meetings, and to remain engaged. This contributes to ongoing frustration with regulatory agencies—employees of the agencies are paid for their work, but residents have to take time out from their other activities.

One activist spoke of having expressed concern about drilling to a co-worker. "She said there was a city council meeting that night and this was one of the things they were going to talk about. I said 'I don't go to city council and complain,' you know? But it was real upsetting to me. I felt like I needed to say something." She went to that meeting, and she is now one of the more active protesters in the Shale. This sentiment—"I don't go to city council and complain"—was a strong part of the reluctant activist's stories as they explained their backgrounds to me.

"This is a bedroom community," another activist said. "Most people that live out here don't ever venture down to City Hall. This is true of a lot of these communities [in the urban areas of the Barnett Shale]. Bedroom communities. They don't even know where City Hall is. City governance is— they're just not aware of it." "Not being involved in your local community," he added, "is a huge factor in all of this and is how [the industry] has been so successful."

Another activist spoke about the difficulty of keeping people involved in activism. People, she noted, are being "lawyered up or they are media fatigued." Should they become involved in a civil lawsuit, they are generally told not to speak publicly about the case, and often a gag order is part of any settlement they receive. Both silencing through the courts and media fatigue serves those in power by cutting the voices of the activists out of the discourse.

"They're tired of talking. [The reporters] pull out your heart for two or three hours and all [they report] is one or two sentences. They are so tired. They're sick of the media," one activist told me.

"It's not fun to go to city council meetings at seven o'clock," another said, "when I can be tucking my daughter in bed. The whole reason I'm doing this is to make this community better for my kids."

One activist said that, after several years of protesting the industry, she felt she could no longer be so involved in the issue. "It was such a disheartening thing to go through," she to me. "After all the years of fight-ing. I've really withdrawn."

"You choose how much of your life you're willing to invest in this," another activist told me, "before you finally say 'I'm done. You can have it. I tried.'"

Activism fatigue translates into the exclusion of citizens from the con-versation about natural gas drilling and reflects the structural barriers to political participation.

In addition, the people in my study suffered from a lack of respect for their environmental identity. Most of them moved to their community because they wanted to live in a rural-like setting with the conveniences of urban life. They were drawn to the green spaces, and they believed that their chosen community was a "good place to raise kids." No doubt these are privileged ideals of the dominant class; nonetheless, this is the environ-mental identity of this group of people. To learn that the "good place to raise kids" is toxic, or that the coveted green spaces are being paved over with industrial equipment, is an assault to their environmental identity. Figueroa's definition of environmental justice thus encapsulates more of this community's experience than traditional theories of environmental justice.

"Early on, I really wasn't concerned—quite honestly—about the health risks," one activist said. "I didn't even think about emissions. I didn't want to live with industrial facilities. Because that's my right. That's my choice. That's what a community [here she pounded on the table for emphasis] is allowed to do with zoning. Make sure they don't live in an area that doesn't embody the values that they're looking to live in."

Through the course of my research, I believe that converse of the tradi-tional environmental justice perspective is that middle-class and upper-middle-class people have a false sense of security when it comes to toxic exposures. This is supported by literature on public perception of air qual-ity. As I have already noted, air quality in the Dallas–Fort Worth metroplex is not good, yet many people who live in the area hold the impression that it is. They are used to buying their way to safety and to living with an envi-ronment that they do not have to worry about. Shocked to attention when they learn they may have something to fear in their environment they find their usual safety mechanisms lacking.

Not in Anyone's Back Yard

"How close a person lives to a heavily polluting industry remains a largely overlooked measure of inequality in the United States," writes Lerner (2012, 297). In the case of natural gas drilling in urban North Texas, middle-class and upper-middle-class communities are being affected by activities related to industrial natural gas extraction. The spaces in the infrastructure are being used for these activities, whether they are green spaces between homes, children's soccer fields, or golf courses. Not all members of the communities are fighting back, but some are. Social capital cannot be used to wash away environmental injustice for the middle class, and one should not assume that all middle-class resistance is a function of NIMBYism. To do so furthers the environmental injustice that middle-class people experience.

My project deviates from much of the environmental justice literature in terms of the standpoint of the activists and their outlook on social activism. The people I studied are largely politically conservative, middle-class to upper-middle-class, and new to activism. Activism was not part of their identity before this experience, and they do not seem to see themselves as in solidarity with other environmental health activists aside from those protesting natural gas drilling.

They recognize and resent the label "Not in my back yard." They view themselves as protectors of not only their own community but also of other communities affected by natural gas drilling. Many see their activism as maternal—in the words of one activist, they are "mothers of the community." They view their activism against natural gas drilling with a sense of altruism—motivations for activism are very important to their burgeoning identity as activists. Finally, reluctance permeates their activism: they would prefer not to be in this world, and feel that they don't really belong in it, yet because of the motivations discussed earlier they are compelled to be in it.

It is important to note that, although the activists share the characteristics just mentioned, there is significant diversity among them. I use the term "activists' for ease of discussion, but, as one respondent said, "there are differences in framing and issues and hobbyhorses and all of that." In addition, none of the participants called themselves reluctant activists; rather, this was a phenomenon that I discovered continually in the data, and that was illuminated further the longer I remained in the field.

When natural gas rigs move into urban neighborhoods, some citizens respond—reluctantly—by becoming environmental health activists. They are suddenly aware of both their embeddedness in the natural world and the fragility of that world. Theirs is not an easy fight.

"There's so many people who just stick their head in the sand," one activist told me. "Even people who live by [gas sites] don't know. I feel like we're being taken advantage of. Companies say everything is fine. I moved into my neighborhood for this school. I feel duped. We bought this house. We put in a pool." She went on to add that through her ordeal she learned that "you can't get away from pollution. So you stay where you are and fight where you live. But you don't know what you're up against."

Ecological Violence

"Over that ridge, there's a subdivision. They've got six tanks, and house, house, house, all facing it. The front of their houses. I just started to wonder, do [the people from the industry] just hate the people out there?" As this quotation suggests, activists repeatedly expressed that the industry possessed an aura of arrogance, supremacy, and untouchability. That arrogance, they said, was validated by the lack of governmental oversight and by laws that favor the industry's practices. "These guys are so arrogant," one activist told me. "They're so confident about the power they've accumulated." What manifests is nothing less than an atmosphere of violence.

What happens when the guardians are not guarding? Many of the activists I interacted with claimed to have been harassed and intimidated by people working for the industry because of their protesting. Repeatedly, activists told me about incidents in which they felt frightened and physically vulnerable. "The biggest story never told in the Barnett Shale is the intimidation," one activist said, adding that "people are so intimidated by the industry." Another activist told me that representatives of the industry had been pressuring her to stop talking. "They've threatened to break my jaw," she said. She told me that people from the industry said that "they're going to take me and my lovelies out Chicago Style," and that she worried that they would "come by and shoot my horses in the pasture or something to retaliate against me."

A number of activists said that they preferred working "behind the scenes" because of fear of retaliation from the industry. A few mentioned reluctance to take part in this research because of fear of reprisal. "I'm in danger," one woman told me. They also try not to have their names made public. Some use pseudonyms on the Internet. They are truly frightened of possible reprisals.

One woman claimed that she heard of industry executives demanding that reporters who had published negative articles about natural gas drilling be fired. Several of the activists reported having been harassed in the comments sections of their blogs or Facebook pages and having received threatening email messages.

According to Shiva (2009), "the eco-imperialist response to the climate crisis is to grab the remaining resources of the planet, close the remaining spaces of freedom, and use the worst form of militarized violence to exterminate people's rights and people themselves when they get in the way of an economy's resource appropriation, driven by the insatiable greed of corporations." Intimidation tactics are clear attempts to silence critics of the industry. Indeed, as I type these words I wonder if I will experience retaliation for them.

Expressions of violence against protesters were raised during a conference of representatives of the natural gas industry held in Texas in 2011. An activist with Earthworks' Oil and Gas Accountability Project recorded and made public a talk given by a gas-industry public relations specialist about how to manage negative media reports about the industry's practices. The talk, titled "Designing a Media Relations Strategy to Overcome Concerns Surrounding Hydraulic Fracturing," specifically referred to the use of "psyops"—military-style psychological operations—by the industry. One news agency reported having "obtained audiotapes of the event, on which one presenter can be heard recommending that his colleagues download a copy of the Army and Marine Corps counterinsurgency manual" (Javers 2011). This advice came from a related session at the conference, titled "Understanding How Unconventional Oil and Gas Operations Are Developing a Comprehensive Media Relations Strategy to Engage Stakeholders and Educate the Public." The speaker instructs the audience to "download the U.S Army-slash-Marine Corps counterinsurgency manual, because we are dealing with an insurgency. There's a lot of good lessons there."

It was not a good day for the gas industry's public relations people.

Sharon Wilson, a representative of Earthworks' Oil and Gas Accountability Project, writes extensively about psyops tactics on her blog, titled Blue Daze Drilling Reform (Wilson 2014). "They [meaning the industry] are calling it a war," Wilson writes. "We are considered 'insurgents.' They employ ex-military PSYOPS personnel in our neighborhoods. They track us and map our relationships." Activists are thus likened to terrorists by some people within the industry and are treated with military tactics. This reads like an act of violence to me.

Absher (2012, 89) conceptualizes ecological violence as both "systematic violence against the people" and "violence that operates in the complex interrelation between people and the environment world they disclose through their practices." This schematic includes both personal violence (physical and mental) and structural violence (social groups and institutions engaged in oppression and exploitation). "You feel almost like you're being stalked," one woman told me

In other cases, the violation is subtle. One activist mentioned to me that he often felt intimidated—"Not because anyone is explicitly threatening you, but the message is sort of in the simple presence of these people that you have done something to get yourself on their radar. And you ought to. . . . There's this unspoken message, right? "

A governmental regulator told me that all of her emails were requested under the Freedom of Information Act by a pro-industry organization in what she believes is an intimidation tactic. This included all correspondence with citizen activists. While less afraid for herself, she was concerned about the activists who had corresponded with her—concerned that they would somehow become targets for violence by the organization. She wondered what the organization was looking for in her emails, and whether it was found.

The activists spoke of feeling traumatized, of the difficulty trying to balance a normal life while fighting an enormous and powerful industry. They often described navigating the spaces in terms similar to those used by victims of disasters—terms suggesting that their world is in turmoil while the rest of the world is unscathed and fine.

Ecological Violence and Mining

Mining operations worldwide have been correlated with conflicts and with human rights violations (Urkidi and Walter 2011). George Leader, a former governor of Pennsylvania, said the following in a 1995 interview:

There is something about the extractive industries that, somehow, exploitation seems to be the only word that applies. They don't seem to care about the hospitals or the churches or the community buildings or even the infrastructure unless it directly affects them. They just never did anything to help the community. They just got in and they took their money and they did as little as they could to protect the workers from dust, from cave-ins, from anything. They just did the minimum. That's what it was all about. Get in[,] get their money[,] and get out. (Goodell 2007, 31)

Study after study has demonstrated that fossil fuel mining is associated with structural violence, conflict, and exploitation (Orta-Martinez and Finer 2010). Researchers have repeatedly documented that mining communities experience increases in patriarchal culture, physical and nonphysical abuse, and alcohol and drug use (all of which are also associated with increases in interpersonal violence and sexual violence) (Nancarrow, Lockie, and Sharma 2009; Sharma 2009.

In their discussion of coal mining, Stretesky and Lynch (2011, 210) draw on a theoretical "perspective that landscapes around strip mining facilities are altered by the demand for coal and the level of environmental oversight that is shaped by a community's economic competition." Normalization of mining activities, they write, "can promote the extension of powerlessness and inequality within a mining community" (ibid., 211).

As was noted in chapter 1, violence was a facet of boom towns early in Texas oil and gas culture. Such violence appears to be a continuing legacy.

Sexual Ecological Violence

Alisha told me about trying to hire an attorney to fight the natural gas company that had come onto her property: "We started telling the attorney our story. And the attorney opened up his desk drawer and he took out a hammer, and he said 'You're going to get screwed. It's your choice whether you want to take it this way [here she mimed holding a hammer vertically, then shifted it horizontally] or this way.'"

Similar to constructions of rape, Alisha said, the attorney went on to say that she and her husband were "just asking for it." "Don't fight them," the attorney advised, "and things will be better for you."

The couple continued to fight the gas company, against the advice of the attorney. Alisha said she called one regulatory agency and had begun to explain her issue when the employee on the other end interrupted her. "I know exactly where you are," he said. "We've been out there investigating before, and we'll be out there tomorrow." The response, Alisha told me, felt menacing, more like a threat than a helpful reply. "Two days later," she recalled, "they knocked my fence down when I wasn't home. I kid you not.

The site supervisor said 'We're thinking about putting two wells out here on your property.' I said 'We only own 10 acres. This is a 950-acre lease. I have no other place to put my horses.'" She said she felt the action was a punishment, in direct retaliation to her protests. She lost. The wells went in.

When the equipment arrived, no one was home. Employees from the company knocked down their fence to bring trucks on to the property, releasing Alisha's horses in the process. A neighbor called Alisha at work to let her know that her horses were running loose. To this day the family has not been compensated for the damage to their property.

"When I came around the corner," Alisha recalled, "there was about a 100-foot section of the fence cut out, a pipe fence. We spent $15,000 on that pipe fence. And they had taken it and flung it to the side." She and the neighbor had to chase the horses to catch them and bring them home.

Violence manifests in different ways in the gas fields. Some is enacted on the land, some on the environment. In addition to pollution and degradation of air, water, and soil, there are concomitant effects on human, animal, and plant life. Violence against protesters, threats, patriarchal control, and silencing the protesters are expressed as physical, emotional, and sexual in nature.

In my study, I found that much of the violence discussed by the activists was sexualized. In an interrogation of sex and the environment, Mortimer-Sandilands and Erickson (2010, 5) write that "there is an ongoing relationship between sex and nature that exists institutionally, discursively, scientifically, spatially, politically, poetically, and ethically." Given such strength of the relationship, it is perhaps (sadly) not surprising to find violence expressed as sexual violence.

The social construction of the outdoors is hypermasculine. Natural spaces are heteronormative, the wildness "an important site for the cultivation of heteromasculinity" (Mortimer-Sandilands and Erickson 2010, 14). This is seen in the language of the oil fields, with "field roughnecks" and "oilmen" working at the sites. Meanwhile, the earth itself is constructed as feminine ("Mother Earth"). She is to be tamed and conquered. Natural resources are framed as commodities, to be taken and sold for profit, just as women's bodies are commodified. These conceptualizations are carried forth in the Barnett Shale discourse, where the industry is cast as masculine conquerors and the activists are feminized, obstacles to overcome in the quest to conquer Mother Earth.

"People are absolutely terrified," one activist told me, "and industry does a lot of stuff to intimidate them. It's just like being raped. If you read [accounts] of what's happened, it's like a rape victim." Indeed, the same metaphor cropped up in my own mind often during interviews.

I dislike rape metaphors, and throughout this project I resisted them. Yet it is difficult to listen to the activists' stories and not think of rape, particularly when the activists themselves make the connections between what is happening to them and the act of being raped. The intimidation they discussed was nearly always gendered and sexualized. I believe there is a sexual component to ecological violence. Sexual metaphors were used so often by the people I spoke with that to exclude them from this analysis would not be authentic.

As much as I would like to, one cannot ignore the 'fracking'/'fucking' wordplay that creeps into the discourse about natural gas extraction. Activists play on the two terms with protest signs bearing such messages as "Get the frack out of my town" and "Don't frack with Texas." And such wordplay seems apt. Natural gas drilling does involve the penetration of the earth with a drill. After penetration, millions of gallons of fluid are ejaculated into the hole, cracking the earth and spreading it open. This crass and obvious metaphor permeates the Barnett Shale narrative. The activists often used that metaphor to describe their experiences in interactions with the industry and with government officials.

"Being the fighter type of people we are, my husband and I put up protest signs on our property," one activist told me. "We put one facing the well site, that said '[gas company] shame on you!' And it was, shame on you for destroying our property. Within two weeks, two people—because there were two footprint tracks—someone trespassed on our property up here and spray painted [the signs] with the picture of female genitalia and then wrote 'pussy' and then the letters 'U R next,' and then the picture of male genitalia. We found that on the way to church on Sunday morning, and my daughter was in the back of the truck." What is the message other than a threat of impending rape?

Rape of the land seems like such a tired metaphor, but perhaps that is the point. Being screwed up the ass with a hammer, being injected with toxins forced through an artificial hole—these images bring up threats of contamination, violence, exploitation, and abuse. This is the language the activists use, this is the metaphor they draw upon to express their violation. Perhaps the use of this metaphor demonstrates that the activists have no other language to describe just how violated they feel. A rape reference seems to resonate with them, and to be the cultural construct that best expresses their pain.

"It's an unfortunate situation," one activist told me. "Reminds me of the gold rush, you know, they're just grabbing what they can and then they're going to leave. Greed, money, power. It's frustrating, because you feel like this little guy, but you know, hey, I'm one person and I've seen little changes. So if everyone does something . . . ."

6   Epistemic Privilege

I sit in a large lecture hall struggling out of my coat when the Texas Railroad Commissioner approaches me. He is working the crowd. He sticks out his hand to shake mine, which is tangled in my sleeve. I try to shake hands, but the movement is awkward, and part of my bra flashes from the neck of my shirt. He ignores my distress (if he even noticed it) and continues along the audience row. The entire exchange exemplifies what activists tell me about their interactions with his agency. Oblivious to my personal struggle, this man is here to get a job done.

The program begins, and the Railroad Commissioner comes to the front of the room to speak. "I'm here to present as many facts as I can," he says. Later in his presentation, he stated "Science and fact are key to what makes the Railroad Commission work." This feels like—and is interpreted as—a slight toward the activists. The unspoken implication is that their knowledge is not in the realm of science and fact. Conflicts over who holds (and wields) epistemic privilege, such as this one, dominate the Barnett Shale discourse.

Epistemic Privilege Defined

Epistemology is a branch of philosophy that deals with knowledge and how we know. Epistemological questions include what constitutes knowledge, whose knowledge claims are dominant, and whose knowledge claims are held as "truth." "Epistemology can be understood as a *justificatory account* of the scientific production of knowledge," Pascale (2011, 4) writes. Epistemology encompasses how we know a thing and how we come to believe what we know. Epistemic questions involve the construction of meaning, how meanings emerge and evolve, and the power relations involved in the

...struction of knowledge (Scott 1988 as cited in St. Pierre 2011). One group's knowledge is said to be privileged when it dominates the discourse, when that group's way of knowing about the world is viewed as better than another group's way of knowing the world. In many conflicts such as those surrounding natural gas development today, science lies at the heart of the dispute (generations ago, religion held this place).

There is a political aspect to the production of knowledge. Pascale (2011, 14) writes that "the way that power is distributed across social, cultural, economic, and institutional orders strongly influences what we have learned to regard as knowledge." One of the major struggles among the activists, the industry, and the regulatory agencies in the Barnett Shale involves epistemic privilege—that is, whose knowledge is "correct" and whose knowledge is prominent in the natural gas discourse. Because each group has a different standpoint, their knowledge about the issues differ— often significantly. The question then is "Which knowledge is listened to and given credence, and which is discounted and considered invalid?" Epistemic privilege is important because public policy is framed and informed by the knowledge that is considered legitimate or "correct."

As I noted in the introductory chapter, my research was guided by the theoretical principles of social representation theory. Groups construct representations about events that are important to them. Construction of a social representation happens in discursive practice. During this practice, facts are identified and debated. And there is no lack of facts in the Barnett Shale narrative. Time and again, facts are shared, and the facts are often contradictory. "Frack fluid chemicals are harmful to human health," one group says. "The volume of chemicals in the fluid is too low to be hazardous," another group says. "People living near the gas wells have high rates of cancer," one group argues. "No," says another, "there is not a statistically significant rate of cancer here." Many news outlets cover pieces of the action, and, as one activist told me, on the Internet it is easy to find evidence to support any perspective. "Environmental issues are almost always contested," Gunter and Kroll-Smith (2007, ix) write, "and are likely to transform communities into volatile places." The evidence is weighted depending on how it is framed, on the goals of the different groups involved in the debate.

Consider a community as embedded in time and space. An object (in this case, natural gas development activities) is inserted into that

community. Members of the community then attempt to make s
that object. They create a representation—a narrative explanation o.
the object fits into their social reality. The representation is considered to
social because it emerges through social interaction, through discursiv
practice, through discussion and counter-discussion, in a variety of textual
and geographic spaces. This type of knowledge construction, however, is
neither neutral nor democratic—more powerful groups dominate this process and silence less powerful voices.

"Facts" shape this process. They are inserted into everyday discourse,
and the community must decide what to do with the influx of new information. "Facts" minus sources are recycled throughout the Barnett Shale
narrative and accumulate and solidify. Some "sound bites" occur over and
over—for example, one that argues that frack water is permanently
removed from the hydrological cycle, one that argues that air quality is
getting better or worse, and one that argues that invasive breast cancer is
on the rise in North Texas. There is little or no acknowledgment of the
sources of this information, or even if the bites are true, behind acceptance
of which argument fits which side. Instead "truth" is slippery, mutable,
and much fought over.

At a town hall meeting, a petroleum engineer with one of the gas companies made this statement: "Proven. It's a known fact that hydraulic fracturing of rock itself has not contaminated ground water." He may as well
have hurled an explosive charge into the crowd of activists. Their facts support the opposite.

Sorting through the myriad facts to uncover one truth is problematic.
"Evidence," Lather (2010, 45) writes, referencing Schwandt (2008), "must
always be interpreted. . . . Interpretations can be flawed; evidence is provi-
sional, revisable, emergent, incomplete, constrained and created, interpreted and judged in communities or inquirers." Criteria and standards
vary by discipline, by the lens used to collect and interpret data. Evidence
is presented to the community and must be sorted and processed.

The social construction of natural gas drilling as an environmental
health threat is an ongoing process. As is detailed throughout this book,
many concerns are open and under debate, and much uncertainty remains.
According to Edelstein (2004, 12), this sort of uncertainty "serves to mag-
nify the significance of the available 'facts' about a contamination
event. . . . The important thing about these 'facts' is not that they are

generally or to some group of experts but rather that they are known ̣e exposure victims." These "facts" become solidified—objectified—in . collective consciousness. Yet in most cases the fact held by the exposure ̣ictims are not validated by the experts (who usually don't reside in the exposure area and have not been exposed). This leads to conflicts, and the victims do not get the help or support they seek.

Fact, Fetish, Factish

One way in which knowledge is controlled in the Barnett Shale discourse is through the use of science. Science is legitimized as the only valid source of knowledge by the people who hold the power to make such a designation— the industry and the government regulators. The debate seems to take on what Latour (2010) described as a fetish/fact dichotomy. In this dichotomy, a fact is defined as knowledge based on scientific practices (science in this case in the utmost sense of positivism), while the fetish is knowledge based in emotion, opinion, or fallacies in reasoning.

Positivism, a philosophical orientation by which knowledge is created through the systematic testing of theory-derived hypothesis, purports to be objective. Through objectivity, human intervention is said to be removed. Positivists strive for truth external to the inclinations of humans. Yet this ideal is highly criticized in some circles. That there is any human involvement whatsoever in the process signals some degree of bias. A human wrote the theory, a human chose the theory to test, a human set up conditions in a certain lab in a certain way—throughout the scientific method, a human makes decisions. That human intervention removes any possibility of true objectivity—all science is a human creation.

There is conflict between the word 'fact' and how people define what makes a fact factual. Are facts reflections of reality independent of humans, or are facts socially constructed, products of human thought? Latour (2010, 16) writes: "Either he has socially constructed his facts out of whole cloth (and thus adds no reality to the world's repertoire other than that of his fantasies, prejudices, habits, or memories), or else the facts are real (but then he did not construct them out of whole cloth in his laboratory)." Here Latour is writing about knowledge and Louis Pasteur's work in the laboratory, but his illustration of constructivism versus realism may be extrapolated to provide insight into the problem of epistemic privilege in natural-gas-related science. Are "facts" socially constructed, or do they have an objective reality?

Complicating matters, Latour (2010, 18) continues as follows:

For [Pasteur], constructivism and realism are synonymous terms. Facts are fabricated . . . but critical thought had trained us to see the fetishism of the object in this ambiguous etymology. Whereas we fabricate them in our laboratories with our colleagues, our instruments, our hands, facts are supposed to become, by some magical effect of reversal, something that no one has ever fabricated before, something that holds up against any change in political opinion, any torment of the passions, something that stays put when someone pounds the table with his fist and shouts: "Here are the facts! They're not going away."

Thus Latour argues that facts are real, in that they exist, but are also constructed, in that human intervention caused facts to be revealed in the first place. There is no objective knowledge, because knowledge is created by humans. Human bias can never be eliminated. This idea is useful for understanding the conflicts in regard to epistemic privilege in the discourse about natural gas drilling. Latour (2010, 21) writes:

The ordinary actor blurts out something entirely self-evident. . . . "We are indeed being manipulated by forces that go beyond us," he might say, tired of being tossed about in all directions and accused of naiveté. . . . The word 'fact' seems to point to external reality, and the word 'fetish' seems to designate the foolish beliefs of a subject. . . . Both conceal the intense work of constructionism that allows for both the truth of facts and the truth of minds.

Those in the pro-drilling camp label the "fetishes" of the anti-drilling and drilling-safety camps unscientific and emotion laden. They call into question the legitimacy of the activists' knowledge claims. They do this by using their own "facts" while leaving the constructed nature of those facts (and thereby their fetish quality) unquestioned. In nearly all cases, members of the pro-drilling camp hold enough political and economic power to protect their own claims.

"Researchers," writes Latour (2010, 23), "are expected to choose between construction and truth, spend every day and many nights in the laboratory constructing truth." Science is itself constructed, yet knowledge that is christened scientific holds the most weight in the conflict over drilling for natural gas.

Interestingly, the pro-drillers often hide behind their own chimeras. While diverting attention toward the naiveté of the activists, they have no "proof" that their activities do not cause harm. They shift the burden of proof off of themselves and onto the activists, the logic then being that if the activists cannot prove that natural gas activities are harmful, they must instead be safe. Thus the import of epistemic privilege—through the entirety of this project I have yet to see anyone from the industry prove that they are not causing harm.

Ultimately both groups have their own factishes—suspensions of conflict between constructionism and realism (Latour 2010). Both rely on constructed knowledge. Yet one group has more power than the other. The pro-drillers hold an epistemic privilege that has nothing to do with quality of evidence.

Neoliberalism, Science, and Policy Making

Epistemic privilege is particularly problematic when the political system relies on science in making decisions. Many researchers argue that the United States has entered a neoliberal turn. Neoliberalism is defined as "a marriage of limited government, free-market, self-correcting capitalism, individualism, and 'traditional' values" (Lather 2010, 11). Decision making is decidedly technocratic: policy is drafted on the basis of expert scientific input. This approach, however, assumes that science is infallible and that it contains all truths. Possible health effects related to extraction of natural gas have come to the forefront of the policy debate. While the industry argues their practices are safe, activists have compiled evidence that suggests otherwise. Decisions are said to be based on science, although as the science of the two groups differs the more powerful group determines the outcome.

Lather (2010) notes that one facet of the neoliberal turn is a reifying of positivist orientations as the basis for sound public policy. She writes of "research as handmaiden to official governmental forces in policy making" (ibid., 5), but it is a particular kind of research that is privileged: evidence-based positivistic inquiry, performed by expert scientists. The findings of this type of research may be counter to the lived experiences of the activists.

Technocratic policy formation assumes an ontology of realism—of a reality knowable by objective scientific method (Savin-Baden and Major 2013) and involving quantification and deductive reason. Although certainly a valid form of knowledge creation, this is not the only way gain knowledge about the world. Yet neoliberal-informed politics privilege such knowledge and devalues other ways of knowing about the world. "Contemporary science," according to Whiteside (2006, 102), "has, in effect, turned the world into a laboratory. Still, it is a laboratory that we all inhabit." As some activists gather this insight, they move toward conducting popular epidemiology (Brown 1992), emulating the legitimized knowledge apparatus. However, as laypersons (and particularly as laypersons will less power), they still are not afforded the prime status of expert science. Their science is viewed by those in power as flawed simply on the basis of their non-expert status.

However, science is a nebulous creature.

Science becomes problematized when one seeks an overriding definition. What is science? Can science be a mode of inquiry other than positivism? Why is positivism itself not subject to the same level of criticism (such as bias and subjectivity) as other forms of scientific inquiry? Indeed, all science is biased. All science has flaws. No science is completely value free. "This," Lather (2010, 33) writes, "is the end of the innocent notion of knowledge production as value-neutral." Lather calls for "a sustained critique of the nakedly self-aggrandizing aspects of this scientistic approach to policy-driven research [that] includes a look at who benefits from federal imposition of experimental trials as the gold standard" (ibid., 42). One must ask who benefits from the reification of positivism.

According to Gunter and Kroll-Smith (2007, 105), "the problem of environments and communities is inevitably linked to languages of expertise. Experts, however, rarely speak with a unified voice." Experts approach their science with the lens of their own discipline, and experts often disagree.

One of the activists I interviewed spoke of the entanglement of science and politics and of how this entanglement obscured other policy considerations: "When is it really a scientific issue, or an engineering [issue], or a legal issue, or when is it just a matter of politics? Also, [there are] ethics and values and justice questions. There's a danger that if you don't raise those explicitly we're always making decisions that are value laden. The dangers of [let's] 'black box' those and treat [the issues] as simply a technical or a legal or an engineering perspective." This activist saw himself as wanting to open that "black box" to raise the ethical and justice issues that are pushed to the side in technocratic decision making.

"Science is and always has been a highly *political* process," Whiteside (2006, 102) writes. "Political, in this context, means that scientists use techniques of persuasion—rhetorical appeals and deliberately staged demonstrations—to win the consent of key actors who will help them make their hypotheses credible."

Brody, Peck, and Highfield (2004, 1571) write that policy makers "cannot rely on scientific data alone to drive a public decision-making process, but also must consider location-based factors, the specific makeup of the population, and the venues through which this population received information about environmental problems." Policy makers have a variety of considerations, and there is a need to allow themselves to be open to a variety of knowledges rather than to be swayed by more powerful voices.

"I'm not a technical person, to be able to prove or disprove," one activist told me. "I'm just saying something's not right." This outlook—that something is not right—this lived experience of harm—should not be discounted because it may not be backed up with expert science. Yet that is exactly what happens in many areas of the Barnett Shale.

Power in Discursive Practice

The importance of power in discursive practice was illustrated during meetings of the Oak Hollow Gas Drilling Task Force, which had been created by the city to advise the city council on changes the residents of the city would like to see to the oil and gas ordinance that was under review. The members of the task force were appointed by the city council. Not all of them were residents of Oak Hollow, and a few clearly represented the industry's interests. They were asked to identify areas within the ordinance that the public wanted the city council to consider, and not to draft any specific changes to the current ordinance. Ultimately, the group worked in an advisory capacity only, and had no real power in regard to the ordinance itself—power was concentrated in the hands of city officials.

"There's this interesting dynamic between concept and language that was going on," one attendee of the meetings told me. "The task force was restricted to concepts. The city should look at 'green completions.' The city should consider 'electric motors onsite.' The city should consider 'recycling.' Right? That's the general idea." The task force was instructed repeatedly that it should identify concepts of interest and should not debate specific scientific language that defined those concepts. Thus, members of the task force could identify "green completion" as a topic of interest, but they were instructed that they could not precisely define what they meant by "green completion." In this case, city officials held ontological power—like the biblical Adam, they got to name and define. The lay public presented words of interest; the city officials conceptualized these words and then determined whether and how the conceptualizations were to be put into practice.

A divide between citizens and experts became evident, the task force representing a lay perspective (despite the fact that its membership included university professors and other professional scientists) while the city played the role of expert.

"What is written into an ordinance? That was the citizen-expert divide," one participant commented. "Citizens know in general what they would like to see. Experts know if and how to make it feasible." Yet these categories were artificial. Those in power—the city officials—had the right and privilege of claiming the expert role. The public was given a semblance of power, but held no real authority. In this case, power resided in the ability to *approve* a final version of an ordinance. Gunter and Kroll-Smith (2007, 129) write that "combining observation and expertise with a calculating reasoning, citizens 'know' their local environment in a quite different manner than the hydrologist, biologist, or epidemiologist sent to study their backyards." But how valued is this knowledge? How welcome is this knowledge in the policy-making process?

The cities in the Shale embraced an ethic of public participation in the ordinance-writing process along a continuum, some seeking little input and others claiming to seek a lot, but ultimately the legal power to make changes at the ordinance level rests with the city council. Beyond that, the city's authority is limited by state and federal legal statutes.

One activist said: "It's gonna come here and it's gonna plop down on us and it's gonna be sort of this nameless force we must live with. This is the system and this is the way it is and this is the way it must be and you must adapt to *it*. We want to push back against that."

Often calls for public engagement in the drafting of city oil and gas ordinances seemed more of a facade, an action required by the city but not terribly useful to anyone.

"The real danger is all of this is really just fluff," another activist commented. "Because it's almost like the staff is waiting, biding their time and then they're just going to set all [our input] aside and say 'What do we actually need to do'? Right? What technically? And they're not being malicious about it. They just have a mindset of 'We're the experts. We know what the parameters are. We're gonna make the thing the way it has to be. And we'll put up with [citizen engagement] but it's really just a light show.'"

Indeed, some Oak Hollow city officials expressed as much to me behind the scenes. They told me that ultimately they would write the ordinance the way they believed it should be written.

Another activist said this: "They [regulatory officials] hold a lot of power because they're the ones that get to determine whether an idea is legally or scientifically defensible." She spoke of a front stage / back stage dichotomy in which on the front stage citizen engagement is emphasized but in the back the officials hold and exercise all of the power and ultimately set the policies they deem appropriate. "It's all backstage work and we don't get to see why or what. . . . The key is when it [the policy] comes back out, we have to ask for public justification of why this or that idea wasn't built in there. And it's not going to be good enough to just say it's not legally defensible. I've talked to enough lawyers now to know there's a wide range of interpretations about what's legally defensible. Or if they just say it's scientifically necessary? What does that mean? What are they really asking?"

Claiming and Framing

One of the biggest frustrations for activists is that their social representation of urban natural gas development tends to be met with skepticism by policy makers.

"The persistence of controversy is often not a natural consequence of imperfect knowledge," writes Robert Proctor (as cited on page 114 of Nichols 2008), "but a political consequence of conflicting interests and structural apathies. Controversy can be engineered; ignorance and uncertainty can be manufactured, maintained, and disseminated." In cases of health, illness, and the environment in the United States, industry is the beneficiary of persistent controversy. Controversy over knowledge defrays responsible practices. The onus of harm is placed on the residents rather than on the industry that is releasing the chemicals into the environment.

One activist spoke about the difficulty of sorting out all of the information about drilling:

I went to an African American health expo in Fort Worth. They opened up a space at one of the high schools for different nonprofits, hospitals, different things to set up booths. [A natural gas company] had a booth there. I took the pamphlets that they had because they had an old African American man on one of the pamphlets talking about how much he loved the benefits that he got from letting the gas company use his land. Drill on his land. And he loves his sprinkler system. I don't know, there's something else. It's so ridiculous, but the whole book was statements from different families [about the benefits of leasing mineral rights].

She talked about how welcome a check from the gas company would be to people living in impoverished neighborhoods. "The choice probably isn't that difficult," she said. "And are the health problems presented to them in their approach? No."

"Facts" are presented in particular ways to influence the social construction of natural gas development, and ultimately to influence public policy. For example, the incident described above took place at a health fair, suggesting and legitimizing a pro-health message. Why would any practice harmful to health be in a booth at a health fair?

"Data" and "facts" come from a variety of sources. In every case, however, one can find contestation of validity and reliability. In the Barnett Shale narrative, scientific authority was constantly questioned. While the activist's science was criticized as anecdotal, the regulatory agencies' science was criticized as biased in favor of industry. Each of the three groups—activists, regulators, and industry—criticized the others' research methods and tried to discredit their findings.

"In every case," one activist explained to me, "whether it's the TCEQ or the industry doing these air tests, or the state health department, you cannot look at the press release or the executive summary. You have to look at the data. You go look at the data and it tells a completely different story." The findings are presented in a way that supports the claims of whoever is making them.

Another activist spoke about the problems associated with using quantitative data to support claims of health effects. One city released figures from a study of the quality of ambient air showing levels of various chemical compounds known to have health effects associated with them. In the report, investigators present averaged figures, having computed them into a relatively smooth time line. The line falls below what the state is considers harmful for human health. In contrast, activists focused on the outliers in the air-quality readings—selected data points, brief in time, at which the levels (without statistical smoothing) jumped above the health effects limits. The city and the activists used the same data set and arrived at two very different claims—the city said the data demonstrated safety; the activists said the same data demonstrated cause for alarm. "We have the same facts," one regulatory official said about these numbers. "We just interpret them differently."

Davis (2002, 53) writes:

The approach of studying a public health disaster in order to find ways to downplay its importance relies on a well-known method of proof that recurs throughout the history of environmental health. Where evidence does not conform to what people would like to believe, just make sure that the facts can be adapted. This adaptation can take many forms. Sometimes no studies are undertaken at all, and assurances are given that whatever had happened was just an act of G-d or a freak of nature. Sometimes the times and places being studied are altered so as to make differences harder to see. The places looked at may be expanded so that big differences between smaller regions cannot easily be seen, or . . . the time being studied may be chosen so as to exclude the longer-term impacts altogether. Other times, people simply stop looking.

Attempting to prove their knowledge claims is a constant battle for the activists. One of them told me: "I had some pictures of a fire in Wise County [one of the counties in the Shale] where some tanks at a well site had caught fire. And one of them, the lid blew off and the news story that came with it said it landed 150 feet away. This is after our ordinance says tanks can be 100 feet from a house. So you know, we had industry—[they told the city council] 100 feet is perfectly safe, and luckily I got to speak second and I said, here's a picture." Another activist told me this: "I'm hoping to engender the people that will just look at this based on facts alone to do this. Because what we have is the industry and the people that support the industry, the legislators who get handed legislation is written by these guys. And then you've got the activists, who use all this anecdotal information without taking the time to really get at the proof." Interestingly, though, this same activist realized that presenting "facts" was not a clear solution. She went on to say: "If you talk to people about facts—of course!—they're going to see what you need to do. What you should do. But you know what? It doesn't work like that at all." Though a rational, "factual" presentation might be more palatable to regulatory officials, she noted, presentation of the facts still did not change policy. I believe this experience is a result of epistemic privilege, and in this case the activist did not hold such privilege. It didn't matter how good her science was. She was viewed as incapable of creating legitimate knowledge because of her location in the power structure.

What constitutes proof differs depending on the audience. A scientist will typically argue that there is no proof of anything, only theories and hypotheses to be supported or refuted. For a judge, proof might be a preponderance of evidence. For a politician, it may be what keeps lawsuits at bay. For a cancer patient, proof may be the wafting scent from the natural gas pad next to her home. The standpoint of the person(s) evaluating the evidence affects the evaluation. Values, assumptions, and bias all influence perception.

Creation of a social representation of a health threat is an unfolding, evolving process of becoming, of creating. It is also one that is controlled by people with the power to dominate the discourse. Those in power have a greater ability to ensure that their argument is at the forefront.

"Being quoted in the newspaper scares me," one activist said. She worried about being misquoted. She told me about one newspaper reporter she regularly emails. "I don't deal with [the reporter] on the phone. [The reporter] is so pro-drilling. He has yelled at me. He has laughed at me. So I just deal with him through email. One time he took part of this sentence, the first part of this sentence and the end of that sentence and it was like [loud sighing noise]. Whole different meaning." In this case, the reporter clearly has the power to shape and dominate the discourse.

At one meeting I attended, activists strategized about what they should do at an upcoming city council meeting. Their focus was on making the "facts" compelling enough to change local policy. "We need evidence," a young woman said. "An analysis of what's been done so far. Review of existing data. We have to make them understand."

Another woman wanted to bring cancer patients to the meeting and have each of them share his or her story with the city council. The rest of the group disagreed.

"No, no," one activist said. "The City Manager told me we need to get past all the emotion." The testimony of cancer patients at the meeting would not be viewed as compelling evidence by the city, the activist explained, but would be seen as emotional and therefore invalid.

"Plus, [the patients] are getting tired," someone said. "For some it's everything they can do to fight their cancer. Their world has been turned upside down. What's their motivation to give up another evening to present at a meeting, where they won't be listened to anyway?"

"The forces against us are big," someone added. "We need proof. The burden of proof is on us." But how best to prove their case?

The conversation revolved around quantitative data. The activists believed that with enough quantitative data they would be able to make their case for a strong ordinance. The lived experience of patients fighting cancer that they believe is a result of living in the gas field would, however, be discounted. Patients' experiences would be rendered invisible at the meeting, because they wouldn't be able to prove that activities related to natural gas caused a particular case of cancer.

In the face of technocratic decision making, the activists draw on popular epidemiology to try to legitimize their arguments (Brown 1992). A popular epidemiology dominates environmental health activism, and there is a blurring of "lay" and "expert."

"'Expertise' is another word for myopia or tunnel vision," one activist said. He then made an analogy:

You never ask, when you're an expert, "What is a road?" Of course you know what a road is. Until a non-expert comes in and says "What is a road? Could public art be part of a road?" And I think the same with this drilling stuff. What actually is the leverage that we have to work with? The space, the room, that we could design this system differently? We need to open their minds a little. What is the technical apparatus for fracking, right? It is what it is and I think the value of citizen input is to braise those assumptions. They go under the guise of expertise, but they're just assumptions. It's not the view on the reality. It's a framing of it, and there's an alternate framing, I think.

The Precautionary Principle

To cope with differences in naming and framing, and problems of epistemic privilege, many activists advocate for embracing the precautionary principle (Gullion, Meiers, and Love 2011). "We cannot say," Davis writes (2002, xvii), "that any one person's disease was caused by this particular exposure to this particular chemical on this particular day. The best we can say with any certainty is that if a particular chemical or group of chemicals were not in the environment, some number out of every hundred people who got sick would have remained healthy, and some number of those who died might still be alive. Is that enough?" The answer to that question depends on your standpoint. A representative of the industry might argue that no one can *prove* that a gas well caused someone's cancer. An environmentalist could then argue that even the *possibility* that it caused that person's cancer should be reason enough to stop the practice.

The precautionary principle is a strategy of prevention (Whiteside 2006). The formulation of this strategy in United Nations Environment Programme's Rio Declaration on Environmental Development Principle 15, developed in 1992, reads as follows:

In order to protect the environment, the precautionary approach shall be widely applied to the States according to their capabilities. Where there are threats of serious or irreversible damage, lack of full scientific certainty shall not be used as a reason for postponing cost-effective measures to prevent environmental degradation. (UNEP 1992)

Whiteside (2006, viii) writes that "the precautionary principle applies especially in situations of environmental risk where by the time unambiguous scientific evidence of a serious problem becomes available, the danger may already have materialized and perhaps become irreversible." As was noted in chapter 3, there is still a dearth of scientific evidence regarding chemical exposure associated with natural gas extraction. The available evidence is ambiguous and highly contested. Accordingly, natural gas development is an ideal case for the use of the precautionary principle.

The precautionary principle has been adopted throughout Europe, and has been incorporated in the French constitution, but has encountered significant resistance in the United States, where policy toward chemicals has been based on risk analysis and on cost-benefit analysis (Whiteside 2006). Positivist science informs such policy, to the exclusion of alternate epistemologies. Whiteside (ibid., 39) cites four conditions that are used to assess and manage risk in this type of analysis:

1. Generally, a technology or practice should be regulated only if there is scientific evidence of its causal connection to an identified problem. Regulation must not be based on hearsay, speculation, or unfounded fear.

2. Studies of the problem must be objective—influenced as little as possible by people's emotions or the preferences of special interest. The

quantification of observations and a reliance on scientific methods of verification are the best guarantee of objectivity.

3. Risk-management decisions should be cost-effective.

4. Ranking options consistently require measuring them on a common scale. . . . One must devise common measures for goods (money or life-expectancy gains) so that as much as possible, quantified risks can be put on a single, ordinal scale.

Unfortunately for the lay public, the scientists often disagree. Science is clearly a problem if one relies on what is sometimes termed "hard" scientific data to support anti-drilling claims. Little peer-reviewed scientific research has been published on health and environmental effects, yet there are many documented claims of harm in media reports and governmental agency reports. Indeed, there is no shortage of such claims (Schmidt 2011). Science is always a work in progress. Positivism, as a discipline, induces theory from collections of data or philosophy and deduces tests of hypothesis. Science is iterative, reflecting back on itself as understanding moves ever forward. But the fact that science is a process should not impede policy making based on even limited understandings. Policy, like scientific knowledge, may be refined with new information and circumstance. To halt the protection of public health under the guise of a need for more science is irresponsible.

Use of the precautionary principle also seeks to deconstruct the expert/lay dualism. Latour (as cited on page 102 of Whiteside 2006) argues that "what the precautionary principle clamors for loud and clear is that, by breaking the link between expert knowledge and action, we finally unleash the forces of inquiry that will allow us to maximize vigilance, puzzlement, and risk taking all at once, in regard to questions that heretofore had been withdrawn from discussion." Policy making about environmental controversies can be restructured from a technocratic decision making orientation to a justice-based orientation. Science can be one component in the discussion (rather than the only component), alongside lived experience, ethics, and social justice.

Environmental illnesses are almost always contested. This contested nature is portrayed in conflicts of representation. Who has the power to define an object as a health hazard? Where is the line between fear and fact? What assumptions are being made?

In addition to the tensions related to standards of proof, there are challenges to fundamental assumptions in research on toxins and human health. Through much of the history of toxicology, the understanding was that health effects depend on the dose: the higher the dose, the more poisonous the toxin. Toxicologists believed that minimum levels could be identified below which no harm would occur. In most cases, the parts per billion of the chemicals identified at or near gas drilling operations are below safety levels established by the Texas Commission on Environmental Quality. Yet toxicologists are learning that this is an unfortunate assumption, and increasingly toxins are being identified that cause damage with long-term, low-dose exposures. Indeed, there is much we do not know about the complex interactions of chemicals and the human body.

Most of the research on hazardous compounds has been occupationally related. When employees are exposed to toxins in the course of their jobs, health impacts can be recorded. In those cases, the source of the exposure is known and is quantifiable. Long-term, low-dose exposure studies are difficult, if not impossible, to find in the literature. To design such a research study, to intentionally expose people to toxins, is unethical.

Health effects from pollution may be long delayed. Nancy Nichols (2008) writes about the contamination of the harbor of Waukegan, Illinois, on Lake Michigan, with polychlorinated biphenyl during her childhood in the 1970s. Yet it was not until adulthood, when her sister was diagnosed with ovarian cancer, that Nichols recognized the connection between the pollutant and health. Through her research, she determined that biomagnification in fish may have contributed to her own infertility. Many of the activists I interacted with wondered what health effects we would see twenty years from now among people living in the gas fields today.

Scientific studies of health effects from chemicals are often inconclusive. There are so many variables that it isn't possible to claim definitively that X causes Y. Untangling this complex web leaves room for questioning, and for the assumption of innocence (that is, an assumption that there is no adverse effect on health until it is proved that there is one), and therefore it isn't likely that anyone will be able to prove that there is an adverse effect. Often the burden of proof rests on the community. Chemical manufacturers certainly have nothing to gain by demonstrating negative health outcomes related to their products. Rather, their goal (simply wise business practice) is to aggressively defend and promote their products.

How deadly is a particular toxin? Most epidemiological studies analyze high doses, such as those experienced by industrial workers or during animal studies. These data are used to determine maximum exposure levels—that is, the levels at which exposed people will die. More difficult to quantify are the effects of low-level exposures, either temporary or long term. For instance, if a person is exposed to benzene at an "acceptable level" every day, will that benzene eventually cause pathology? Even more difficult to quantify are the cumulative effects from multiple sources—for example, benzene from the cigarette smoke someone breathed in at a bar, benzene from the auto exhaust someone breathed during his or her daily commute, or benzene wafting from the gas pad next to someone's home. Did any one of these exposures cause harm? Did all of them?

In view of all these questions, science itself is "cherry picked" by various interest groups to support their cause. Kabat (2008, 6) writes:

Given the inherent difficulty of establishing credible links between low-exposure to environmental toxins and chronic disease, it is hardly surprising that the assessment of potential environmental health hazards is hotly contested and that there is a sharp antagonism between the proponents of unfettered freedom for commercial enterprise and those concerned with protecting the public's health and improving occupational safety. Each side tends to cite the evidence that supports its point of view in order to influence public policy.

And because of power relations, ambiguity has historically favored industry.

"The forces against us are big," one activist told me. "They want absolute proof. That *this* benzene from *this* well is doing *this*." This level of proof, however, is impossible to achieve.

The dominant Western biomedical model of illness has emphasized individual lifestyle choices and behaviors and genetic predispositions to chronic ailments to explain disease. Environmental and structural factors have largely been excluded from this paradigm. Thus, illnesses deriving from environmental and structural sources are contested because of "scientific disputes and extensive public debates" (Brown 2007, xiv).

It is difficult to measure chemicals in the body, particularly because of how the body metabolizes different substances. Exactly what should we measure? Should we test for the substance itself, or for its metabolite? How long does the toxin itself remain in the body before it is broken down and excreted? Unfortunately, science and technology are not always able to give a ready response. We know, for example, that the levels of metabolites of DDT (the pesticide dichlorodiphenyltrichloroethane) in the body decrease over time, making it impossible to say with certainty what the burden of exposure to an individual was. One metabolite of DDT is dichlorodiphenyl-dichloroethylene (DDE). Does focusing on DDE skew findings about exposure to DDT, or does it inform them?

"A number of compounds known to induce mammary tumors in rodents—what would be breast cancer in humans—do not leave any traces at all minutes after exposures have taken place," Davis notes (2002, 172). This includes benzene. One activist told me that a physician found evidence of benzene in her teenage daughter's blood. A few months later, the activist got a second opinion from a physician who found no evidence of the toxin in the child's body. Though one hopes the initial result was a false positive (which is indeed the opinion of the second doctor), it is quite likely that the initial findings were accurate and the child had since cleared the benzene from her system. If that is the case (and whether or not it is can't be proved), damage has already been done to her system.

The research is complicated not only by the dose but also by the timing of the exposure—for example, fetal, infant, prepubescent, or pregnant. Exposures at different points in life translate to different effects. Synergy is yet another complication: in the presence of one chemical, another chemical (even one generally considered benign) can morph into a more deadly form.

Further complications arise from the distinction between area source pollution and point source pollution. A point source is clearly identifiable—for example, perhaps a gasoline leak at a particular gas station, on a particular day, created a particular exposure. Most exposures, however, are results of area source pollution—that is, the culmination of all sources of pollution in a particular geographic area. In a large urban zone such as the Barnett Shale, there is no way to distinguish area source pollution from point source pollution.

The picture is further muddied by the victims. "As toxic victims become preoccupied with health concerns," Edelstein writes (2004, 73), "past and current symptoms are attributed to the exposure. Given the delayed onset of environmental health problems, expectations about the future are captured by what victims believe will happen as a result of exposure." People who believe they have been exposed to toxins may have heightened anxiety about their future health, and may wonder whether they or members of their families will get sick or die early. Preexisting health problems are often reinterpreted as deriving from the environmental hazard, particularly problems that were not readily explainable. Illness is now clouded with the uncertainty about chemical exposure.

Peer Review

Expert knowledge is epitomized by peer-reviewed publications. In the Barnett Shale narrative, peer-reviewed publications are privileged, and sound bites seem to be better tolerated when cited from peer-reviewed sources. One method that all the groups involved in this debate used to support the legitimacy of certain facts was to find supporting articles in peer-reviewed scientific research journals.

A peer-reviewed journal has scientific articles submitted to it evaluated blindly by experts in the subject matter. An article must be approved and must meet stringent guidelines before it is published, and it can be quite difficult to have an article accepted.

Peer review has its own politics, some having to do with the process of peer review itself, some having to do with differences in quality of journals, and some having to do with journal articles making the leap from small esoteric circles of like-minded scholars to the public at large. Though many of us long for that leap, it seldom happens, and most articles in academic journals will be read by only a handful of people, many of whom are searching for quotations and references for their own literature reviews.

Peer review takes time, and natural gas development far outpaces scientific advancement. Privileging peer review is accepted practice in scientific circles, but is problematic when it comes to policy making. Peer review is a time-consuming process. I, for example, collected data for a project during the autumn of 2011. I wrote an article using the data during the spring of 2012 and submitted it for peer review. The paper went through the process, was accepted for publication in December of 2012, and was published in the autumn of 2013. Such lags are typical in academic publishing, but are unreasonably long for policy decisions. Suppose the observations I collected during the autumn of 2011 had had serious implications for public health. How much preventable morbidity and mortality would have occurred during the time between observation and publication? Policy makers must rely on the best information available at the time, and that information may not be as solid as one would hope. It may be contested. Policy makers must act anyway, knowing that they can revise their policies later as new information comes to light, rather than delaying waiting for proof that may never come.

Some voices call for peer review of all scientific work on natural gas development before evidence derived from that work is judged (Revkin 2012). Others argue that preliminary findings should be considered and shared.

At one meeting I attended, an EPA report on water contamination in Pavillion, Wyoming was presented as evidence that fracking could cause contamination of well water. The response from the gas industry and from regulators was that the study in question was preliminary and hadn't yet undergone peer review. The evidence was discounted even though the study had been performed by experts who had used a detailed, validated research method.

Government-conducted research, including research presented in official reports, does not undergo traditional peer review unless it is published in scientific journals. The Texas Department of State Health Services report on cancer in Flower Mound mentioned earlier was not peer reviewed. No independent expert reviewed the method or the findings. The monitor of rigor varies between agencies. Some agencies will have multiple internal reviews conducted before research is made public, others few if any.

Whether or not government reports are accepted as legitimate evidence depends more on the characteristics of the audience than on the quality of the research. Thus the same pro-drilling groups discount the EPA's Pavillion study while accepting the findings of the DSHS cancer study. And activists do the opposite.

It is problematic for policy makers to rely on positivist, peer-reviewed research to support anti-drilling claims. Little work on the health or environmental effects of gas drilling has been peer reviewed and published, and the work that has been peer reviewed and published is contested. And though many mentions of documented instances of harm may be found in media reports and in governmental agency documents, such evidence is often deemed "unscientific" and discounted.

It is an ongoing theme in this discussion that ambiguity favors industry. Yet even though the science may be weak or inconsistent, the social representation nonetheless can become concrete. "In the absence of studies conducted to establish statistical significance," Nichols writes (2008, 132), "sometimes we must listen to stories and investigate patterns they may hold." Indeed, this is what the grassroots activists in the Barnett Shale are doing. They are using those stories to construct a social representation of natural gas drilling as a health hazard, and they expect regulatory agencies to act accordingly.

Frackademics

Despite multiple calls from health activists and from the industry for more peer-reviewed studies and more science, academics who inserted themselves into the fracking debate found themselves saddled with the moniker "frackademic." Many found their work maligned in cyberspace—see Revkin 2012 for an example. Questions about their character and their motives were raised, and more than a few careers were threatened. Academic freedom itself came under fire.

"Frackademic" seemed to be a label for academics whose research was used by the natural gas industry to support their claims; however, it was occasionally used to signify any academic who engaged in research related to natural gas. This was an interesting change from academic-activist partnerships often found associated with environmental-health activism. In earlier contested environmental conflicts, activists identified academic allies to help legitimize their knowledge claims. In this case, though, academics were not always well thought of. There are a number of major universities in the Barnett Shale, and in some of these communities there is a history of conflicts between the university and the residents. This may be a contributing factor to some of the distrust of academics. On a larger scale, encapsulated in the neoliberal turn is a "paradoxical dependence on and suspicion of experts and expert knowledge" (Lather 2010, 25).

"Academia is . . . wow. Gee whiz. What a disappointment. It's the egghead Ivory Tower," one activist told me. On the other hand, the same activist said "We really need academic voices. We need a lot more academic research." I believe that this tension between disdain for academics and calls for more academic work stems in part from the institutionalized character of scientific writing. We scientists tend to avoid absolutes, as I often do in this book. We couch our findings in doubts and limitations, and we seldom cross the boundary between what we find in the course of our research and what we should do about it. We prioritize objectivity and discount emotionality. Science is viewed, or is at least presented, as dispassionate. Even when scientists recognize bias in the practice, they often attempt to maintain a distance from politics. This tendency can be a source of frustration for activists searching for an authoritative, powerful voice to say "This is wrong."

Whose voice is listened to in the discourse of natural gas drilling? I am inclined to support Latour's (2010, 20) insight that "social explanations may not have been worth much, but objective causality was no better" and that "we had to go back to square one and start listening again to what the ordinary actor was saying." Science is one form of knowledge—one that has provided great insights into the world and has led to great advancements. But there are other valid forms of knowledge, including lived experience. These should inform environmental controversies, along with concerns about environmental justice and equity. The cacophony of voices may be loud, but no one living in the gas fields should be rendered invisible because his or her knowledge doesn't fit into the dominant discourse. Sometime deviance from the dominant discourse provides society with new insights and new directions.

"It kind of makes your heart hurt a little bit," one activist reflected. "Because no official body has said there's a problem here; in fact, the health department specifically said there is not a problem here."

7 Performative Environmentalism

A young woman approaches the lectern. She is dressed in black, her face painted the white of a skull, with darkened, hollowed eyes and lips. She leans in to the microphone and says: "Hello everyone. I am Death and I'm here to thank you."

A man on the dais interrupts her to ask "Will you please state your name and address for the record?"

The woman complies, but with the interruption Death has lost some of her charisma.

"So, as I said, I am Death and I'm here to thank you," she continues.

"First of all, thank you for not taking the safety of our community seriously. Thank you for appointing several individuals . . . that are associated with natural gas companies on our task force. Companies that consistently distort the truth. Thank you for allowing less than 1,000 feet between our homes and frack wells. Wells that could easily explode. Thank you for not establishing a methane monitoring program. Thank you for putting very few safeguards to protect surrounding communities from accidents and leaks. Thank you for basically ignoring the harmful air emissions that pollute communities surrounding drilling operations, compressor stations and pipelines. Thank you for allowing water contamination from substandard drill casings. Thank you for making only a few of your meetings public. So, that residents of [your] community have hardly any input on issues concerning the safety of their city. Thank you for ignoring the negative health effects associated with natural gas drilling. Thank you for allowing a corporation to bully our community. Thank you for ignoring climate change. The pollution associated with fracking, such as carbon dioxide, accelerates the effects of climate change. And one last thing, thank you for making my job, as Death, easy." (We Are Power Shift 2012)

During the young woman's talk, the men on the dais squirm; the one woman is attentive. One man scribbles on a paper in front of him, the task appearing to consume all his attention. Another gives the audience a bored blank stare. None of them seem frightened of Death's wrath.

Death gathers the pages of her speech and sits back down. The committee moves on.

Activists express the pain and suffering they experience as residents of an environmental sacrifice zone through performative environmentalism. They perform their pain in differing ways, and these performances are a large factor in the social construction of natural gas drilling as a health threat.

Denzin (2003) has argued in favor of a "performance turn" in the social sciences, particularly in light of performativity as public pedagogy. "Performances and their representations," he writes (2003, 12), "reside in the center of lived experience. We cannot study experience directly. We study it through and in its performative representations." Through the spectacle of life, private troubles manifest in public performance.

Performance in sociology traces its historical roots to Mills' (1959) conceptualization of the junctures of biography and history, through "interpretive inquiry," through storytelling and other narrative forms (Denzin 2011, 31–32). "We want performance texts that quote history back to itself," Denzin writes (ibid., 38)—"texts that focus on epiphanies, on the intersection of biography, history, culture and politics, turning point moments in people's lives."

Goffman (1959) envisioned much of social life as dramaturgical. He argued that people actively engage in constant impression management. Using the theater as a metaphor, Goffman conceptualized dramaturgical activities as encompassing both a front stage and a back stage. The front stage is "that part of the individuals' performance which regularly functions in a general and fixed fashion *to define the situation* for those who observe the performance" (ibid., 22, emphasis added). Through performance, then, the activists in the Barnett Shale seek to define their situation, to express their pain about this environmental controversy, and to define the events in light of their pain.

People use performance as a tool for making meaning. Performance is used to transcend boundaries, to bring people into a different world, so that they might understand the lived reality of another group (and perhaps enact empathy). The sociologist Sam Richards (2010) refers to this practice as *radical empathy*: If I can show you what it is like to be in my shoes, perhaps you will be compelled to intervene, to help me. Performance is embodiment of social justice, and is a representation of the lived body (Leavy 2009). "Performance," Madison (2012, 165) notes, "has become a popular signifier expanding the definitions and assumptions of a range of social phenomena. The power of performance is captured in the idea that human beings are naturally a performing species." When we perform, we reveal our Selves, we "simultaneously recognize, substantiate, and (re)create ourselves as well as Others through performance" (ibid., 166).

"We inhabit a performance-based, dramaturgical culture," Denzin writes (2003, x). "The dividing line between performer and audience blurs, and culture itself becomes a dramatic performance." Social activism in the Barnett Shale is enacted through protests, through the writing and telling of stories, through video and film, through speaking in public meetings—through performative acts. "Nietzsche suggests that the central task for human beings is not the Socratic one of making knowledge cerebral and rational," writes Flyvbjerg (2011, 24), "but instead one of making it bodily and intuitive." Through the performance of pain, environmental activists seek to embody their knowledge—that which they embody themselves—in others. They seek to elicit radical empathy. Through performance, they attempt to convey the depths of their pain, its context, its experience. This is a powerful medium. Unfortunately, it tends to be discounted in the discourse because of the primacy of science as epistemology.

Performing Pain

There is a woman who brings a life-size dummy with her to the meetings. The dummy is dressed in overalls and a checkered shirt. The woman sits him in a chair next to her. He wears a gas mask on his face. She calls him Ben—short for Ben Zene. He is the embodiment of the cancer-causing chemical that hovers at gas sites, a reminder of the association between benzene and natural gas pads.

"Where science does not reach," Flyvbjerg writes (2001, 18), "art, literature, and narrative often help us comprehend the reality in which we live." Performances such as the one described above are expressions of the lived reality of the activists. They are expressions of pain. Pain is performed in a multitude of forms: Collective sign holding. Blogs and Facebook pages. Newspaper editorials. Speaking at regulatory and city council meetings. Local bands sing about the problem. Artists construct visual and auditory representations of their pain. Filmmakers create and share videos. Rational voices. Theatrical voices. Shared voices. Voices that whisper and scream "This is wrong. Help us."

"You have to make sure that you're loud enough that people at City Hall can hear you," one activist tells me. We stand on a sidewalk in front of City Hall, facing traffic, holding signs that read "Moratorium on Gas Drilling NOW" and "Cough Cough The Children Can't Breathe" and "Don't Frack With Mother Nature." Cars honk at us. A driver flips us the bird. A woman shouts through a megaphone, berating the city council and the mayor for polluting her city.

Performances of pain in a toxically assaulted community, Pezzullo writes (2007, 11), involve "pain that some answers are not definitive, pain that some ways of knowing have not protected us, pain that some people are dying from this uncertainty and set of assumptions, pain that other people are not, pain that our air, water, and land are suffering to a degree that we have yet to comprehend."

But Is Anyone Listening?

One of the most prominent themes across my study was that activists' performances did not draw a corresponding response from regulators. Widespread radical empathy was not forthcoming. It was as if no one was listening to the people who feel that gas drilling is harmful to public health—as if no one believed them.

The more emotional the performance, the less likely it was to get a positive reception from the regulatory officials. Hung up on "science" as the proper form of expression, they considered the information delegitimized when emotion entered into a presentation. Calm, rational arguments (preferably peppered with figures and references) were better tolerated, were more palatable, than theatrics. "'Objective' science," Pezzullo writes (2007, 11), "remains taken more seriously than admittedly more subjective humanities, rational norms of debate continue to be privileged over more overtly emotional testimonies of experience, and the written word is persistently fetishized in contrast to oral performances." This was the case for the activism I witnessed. Emotionality was equated with kookiness, or even with mental illness—"That woman is crazy," one activist would sometimes say of another.

Science, in the context of the natural gas debate, seemed to be characterized by a lack of emotional engagement. Rationality was privileged not only by the regulatory officials but also by some of the activists. "People get angry and they say things, and just, like, just present the information. Don't be emotional about it," one activist said. To "get emotional about it" signified loss of credibility across groups—among many of the activists (particularly those who had been involved in activism the longest and had already been socialized to *behave properly* though previous interactions and experiences), industry representatives, and regulatory officials. This is despite the fact that theatrical, emotional responses are genuine expressions of pain—people's pain was discounted primarily because of the unpalatable, uncomfortable presentation. These performances made the regulatory officials squirm.

"Attack" tactics seemed to shut down communication between the involved parties. Vibrant expressions of anger, of frustration, of pain, and of fear did not seem to serve their intended purpose of inciting action.

At a town hall meeting, an activist said the following:

There was the one [town hall meeting] the EPA did last year that was like 600 people showed up to, and it was so, you know, you're trying to present the evidence why the EPA needed to study hydraulic fracturing and the emotions became so involved in almost like everybody against industry, and I don't think anything productive really came out of it.

Pezzullo (2007, 73) writes about the problem of certainty and pain. People in pain are fully aware of their suffering. Their pain is real to them. But there is always a haze of uncertainty for the observer—pain is subjective. How does one objectively measure pain? "Because we do not feel pain ourselves," Pezzullo writes, "we are challenged to confirm its existence." Thus we see pain scales in doctor's offices—on a scale of one to ten, where one is feeling great and ten is being actively mauled by a bear, how much pain are you in? (See Brosh 2013.) We hear parents ask their children "Are you *sure* you're sick, or do you just not want to go to school?" We question pain in others because we cannot accurately quantify pain.

Thus, pain is easily discounted by those not experiencing it.

The discourse about natural gas activities is controlled such that expressions of pain are limited. One regulatory official told me:

I love the opportunity to share my experience, share my knowledge, and maybe help people better understand the process. Because I think it slows things down if you're going to a public meeting or you're going to a private forum and you're sharing ideas and you get distracted with conversations that are maybe off topic or poorly focused.

In this case, the performance of the regulator sharing his experience was legitimized through his position as a credible expert—he saw part of his role to be instructing others on proper behavior. Deviant behavior was discounted as "off topic" or "poorly focused," despite whatever perspective the other participants held. This particular official also told me that "distracting emotion" could be removed from the discourse through public education. His educating, his facts, were right and proper, and other forms of expression did not have value. This stance discounts real pain.

Another regulatory official said:

I've had people tell me I'm a bad father. That my home needs to explode. People have threatened my dog, threatened my life. And I'll take those calls and be like, ok, I think they may be concerned. I take that as a challenge because I know there are issues. I know there are concerns. I know there are real threats out there. But if you're that angry thinking that somebody's not doing something, or that the unimaginable to going to happen then I think as a public person, in a public position, I think I have failed you. *Because you don't have good information and it's not really productive if we're trying to have a meeting and we schedule two hours and we spend an hour and forty-five minutes getting people's frustrations out. That is not helping.* If we can spend two hours hearing their concerns, giving them information, so we can have a productive meeting, I think that is more valuable.

A productive meeting, then, is one in which the participants are all well behaved according to the regulator's definition. No discomfort is caused to the officials, the officials are heard, and members of the (passive) public are informed that their pain *is not real*. Thus, performance of pain is discounted by those in power and seems to have an effect opposite to what is intended—it discounts what the performance is expressing.

Physical and Social Space in Environmentalist Performativity

The geography of performative environmentalism is fluid, and physical space shapes and controls both the social interactions and the expressions of performance. Physical space can be a powerful tool for social control.

Participatory democracy is affected by how connected the actors are to the space, how welcome they are, how they are positioned within the space, and the physical and social structures of the spaces in which they interact. These spaces are multiple, and their accessibility varies. They are formal, informal, and electronic. Some of the people involved enter these spaces as employees, transforming them into "work space." Others enter the spaces anew, as "foreigners." They adapt to the spaces and the spaces adapt to them. Belonging or foreignness to the space influences one's being within the space, one's actions, one's confidence, and one's span of influence. Should they stick with the process, activists tend to become more comfortable in it, more a part of it, more a member of the space, understanding and adapting to the space's rules and social realities.

Formal spaces include public meeting areas, such as city council halls and meeting rooms in government and university buildings. These tend to be the most prominent, visible spaces in which natural gas activism occurs. Such places are, by definition, the most public places in which natural gas activism occurs, and perhaps the most interesting in terms of social control. Informal spaces include restaurants, coffee shops, and homes where activists meet and strategize. Electronic spaces are also important, as much of the discursive practice happens in these spaces. These spaces may be public, such as the use of blogs or newspaper websites (through comments); semi-private, such as Facebook groups and listservs; or private, such as email.

An example of the importance of physical space in shaping interactions is provided by a meeting of the Texas Commission on Environmental Quality that I attended—a meeting on air quality that natural gas activists had planned to protest. As I mentioned in the introduction, the protest was held outside the building in which the meeting was to occur. Protesters were sequestered into a courtyard that was not visible from the main road in front of the building. This was during the summer, and temperatures were above 100 degrees. Police in uniform ambled about the space, an unspoken signal for the activists: Don't get out of control or you will be taken away in handcuffs.

Two tents were set up. Under one, someone had placed a variety of literature on a couple of card tables. They placed rocks on the piles of paper to keep them from blowing away. Under the other tent, some of the activists served lemonade and cold gazpacho. The heat was unbearable; I felt rivulets of sweat rolling along my back, and the ice in my lemonade quickly melted (although I was quite grateful for the drink).

During the protest, all of the regulators from the TCEQ were inside the building. They could not see the event from their vantage point. The protest was placed where it would have been highly unlikely for anyone to have stumbled upon it.

About thirty activists attended the protest. A few people spoke using a megaphone. They stood on a low concrete wall that surrounded a dry brown flowerbed. The explained their stories about living in the gas fields and about their fight against the industry. One man detailed the health problems he and his family developed after a natural gas well was drilled in his neighborhood. Several people held poster boards with anti-gas slogans. I became so hot I felt nauseated. I did not see anyone from the media at the event.

After the protest we filed inside for the meeting. Our sweaty bodies shivered in the air conditioning.

The meeting was held in an auditorium. A table was set up at the front of the room for four officials from the TCEQ. A court reporter was positioned to their right. We were instructed that this was a public hearing—the officials would "hear" us. They would not speak to the audience other than to direct the proceedings, nor would they respond to any of the comments.

In order to comment, a person was required to fill out a half-page card, indicating what he or she wanted to say and giving his or her name and address. The comment cards were available at a table in the hallway outside of the room that was overseen by more TCEQ personnel. Once the card was filled out, it was given back to the TCEQ personnel, who carried it over to the court reporter. The court reporter called names for people to speak and monitored the time. No one was allowed to speak more than five minutes.

When a name was called, the person would walk down a central aisle, step up to a lectern equipped with a microphone, give his or her legal name and address, speak, and then return to his or her seat. Then the next name would be called. There were no comments, feedback, or discussion allowed about what someone had just said. About a hundred people sat in the audience, and from the comments it was clear they were diverse in their interests and agendas.

These physical spaces controlled the dialogue and the interaction. The police presence and the court-like meeting room seemed like a threat for the public to abide by expectations of calm and civility. It was almost as if the public were on trial, that they had done something wrong and were defending themselves to TCEQ personnel who sat in judgment. Forcing the protest outside during the summer in a largely hidden courtyard limited the potential audience. As the TCEQ employees could not see the protest and no members of the media were present, the protesters were, essentially, preaching to the choir.

The order of speaking was controlled via the comment cards. The time for speaking was limited, and many people were cut off mid sentence and asked to sit back down. Requiring personal information from each speaker was intrusive. Making speakers walk up to a lectern in front of a crowded auditorium was intimidating. But perhaps the worst part was the passivity of the employees from the TCEQ.

The regulators sitting at the table remained, for the most part, passive and expressionless. At times they read papers in front of them or scribbled on notepads. They occasionally checked their phones. Sometimes they stared off into space. Seldom did they make eye contact with the speakers. Their lack of engagement and response seemed to increase the ferocity of the performances of the protesters, and the presentations became increasingly theatric over the evening to get some sort of response, some sort of empathy from the regulators.

I felt bad for the regulators. They were mid-level employees following instructions. They were not decision makers. Aside from their directive to "hear" and record comments, they seemed to have no power to do anything even if moved by the performances.

The comments presented that night were transcribed and were made available on the agency's website a few weeks later. The event seemed like a charade, a necessary but unwanted detail in the process. But perhaps I am wrong.

Configuration of the space of action can encourage and/or limit interaction. How welcome a person feels in the space influences his or her ability to engage in the discourse. Factors such as the availability of parking and the adequacy of seating and lighting also serve to foster or quell social interaction. The physical positioning of the speakers, who can speak, when, and how all influence discursive practice.

The meta-space of the community matters. Becoming an activist necessarily involved seizing the right to be in these protected spaces and give voice to one's concerns.

Toxic Tours

Our car creeps along a narrow road. I take photographs through the glass—Lindsay has asked that I not roll down the windows, as she gets horrific headaches after she comes out here. We approach a Rockwellesque barn painted in soft blues and whites. From the highway, it appears that what we are approaching is a wealthy yet still somehow quaint farm.

The barn is a facade.

As we meander behind it, we see that it hides pipes and other industrial equipment from the view of drivers on the highway. A hill slopes at the back of the facade, leading to an open concrete space—a well pad, with pipes and tanks and motors and trucks.

A diesel truck hauling thousands of pounds of frack flowback barrels toward us. There is not enough room for it to pass, and Lindsay is forced to drive the car off the road and into the weeds.

Lindsay tells me that for a while the company had hoses similar to fire hoses running across this road. "I guess they were bringing in water to frack here," she says. "But it was all above ground. The crap was leaking, so I really hoped it was just water. I got a great [photograph], in the late winter, so none of this vegetation was here, of cows walking on top of the pipes."

"Am I going to eat those cows?" I asked.

"Yeah." She pulls into the main drive into the gas pad. I hop out of the car and take photos.

"I went to this EPA public hearing in Fort Worth last July, and people from all over EPA Region 6, including Louisiana and Arkansas were there," Lindsay tells me when I get back in the car. "And this man, clearly a downhome, redneck Cajun boy, he went to tell us that they drilled on his property and all of a sudden seventeen of his cows died. So obviously they must have drank something, somehow they got into something." As we drive, she tells me story after story about her experiences as an anti-gas-drilling activist.

As we drive past pad sites, Lindsay points out home after home after home and tell me of the maladies of the occupants—for example, the woman who lives here has thyroid cancer; a child who lives there has leukemia; the family that lived there moved out because the wife was losing her hair just as the woman across the street had. Here are the places, this is what gas operations look like, what they sounds like, what they feel like, here is the air monitor—see how there is a building between it and the frack site, see how difficult it would be to get a valid reading? See the open pits, see the diesel trucks, the hundreds of diesel trucks, see how all the trees on the fence line are dead? See how the drill towers over the soccer field? See it all. See my pain. See me. I'm hurting. We are hurting. Don't you see? Now understand. Help me. Help us.

Toxic tours are another type of performative environmentalism. In many environmental controversies, it is common for activists to show reporters and researchers the physical sites of the polluting industry. I found going on toxic tours myself to be eye opening—it is one thing for someone to explain that the compressors are loud; it's another thing to hear them, or to stand on a football field and calculate that, if I were athletic enough, I could kick a ball into a driller's staging area. To see and feel the short distance between the sites and the homes, and to smell the fumes. After one such tour, I had a headache the rest of the afternoon, and I experienced the first nosebleed I'd had in more than a decade. I could not help but wonder about the cause.

During a toxic tour, Pezzullo (2007, 6) writes, "typically one or more 'guides' walk or drive block to block, pointing out where polluting industries are located in relation to the residents, stopping to allow the 'tourists' to witness the stories of various residents' ailments and struggles, and providing information they have gathered regarding the violations and the apparent effects of these industries on the surrounding land and people."

"By *showing* participants what they believe to be the problems of toxic pollution through *doing* a tour," Pezzullo observes (ibid., 186), "toxic tours embody a performance-centered approach to environmental decision making."

Power, Control, and Performativity

At one city council meeting, groups of activists that were technically "on the same side" chose divergent approaches to the presentation of their concerns. One group (notably made up of activists who were older, both in age and in length of involvement in this issue) calmly presented their "facts" to the city council. Theirs was a reasoned, calculable argument, complete with numerical data and engineering and legal citation. In contrast, the second group (younger and newer to activism) took a confrontational, accusatory response. They berated members of the city council for their inaction and their failure to respond to citizens' complaints. Many of them held up protest signs. After the meeting, not only did members of the first group accuse members of the second of discrediting the entire argument; in addition, city officials rebuked members of the first group for not "controlling" the second group, as if it were their duty as community elders to do so. Regulators consistently attempted to maintain control over public spaces.

A number of groups hosted "town hall meetings." These meetings were characterized by having a supposedly neutral expert (or several of them) present information to the community. These were hosted by a variety of entities: regulatory agencies, grassroots organizations, universities. Despite the appearance of neutrality, however, these meetings had an agenda, whether pro-industry or anti-industry. Often they were framed as if they furthered democracy, allowing for an open exchange between all parties; in practical terms, however, such an exchange did not occur. At most of these meetings (as at the TCEQ hearing mentioned above), in order to comment, a person first had to sign in on a sign-up sheet or fill out a comment card. He or she was then asked to come to a lectern at the front of the room, state his or her name and address, and then speak for a strictly limited amount of time. (Some people were cut off in mid sentence.) Sitting at a table at the front of the room, almost like a panel of judges, sat representatives from the agency. The waiting audience sat behind the speaker, in stadium-style seating. This was the typical format of public comment meetings. The settings were sterile, cold, and intimidating, and generally resembled a courtroom. (In fact, some of the meetings were held in actual courtrooms.) Often a court reporter was present and transcribing. Other times the proceedings were videotaped.

Many of the speakers balked at having to give their name and address— while the public officials were afforded privacy in place of residence, citizens must make this public to have their comment heard. Officials typically did not make eye contact with the citizen speaker. They often instead wrote in a notebook on the table in front of them or fiddled with an electronic device. Greater lack of engagement on the part of the officials seemed to correlate with heightened emotional responses on the part of the citizens, as if they were trying to capture the officials' attention. Anger, name calling and showboating by the activists were common—as if only they could express enough pain to finally capture empathy. When that failed to garner a response, some turned to attack. "How do you live with yourself?" they would ask. Or one alarming soft-spoken comment: "It wasn't that long ago we had lynch mobs in Texas."

The activists were slowly socialized by the regulatory officials and by one another to change their tactics—to embrace a cold rationality rather than a heated emotional exchange. Though the calm, rational approach seldom made much difference in policy outcomes, most of the people involved seemed more comfortable with that type of exchange regardless of what side of the debate they were on.

Pain is performed in numerous ways in the Barnett Shale, but many people are uncomfortable with these performances. After all, who wants to be the *cause* of someone else's pain? Thus, activists' performances of pain are discounted both by those in power and by other activists, and their effect seems to be the opposite effect of what is intended—such performances close communication. Performance is the embodiment of pain, but performances are embedded in structures of power and privilege, structures that shape both the performance and the outcome of the expression. Discourse is shaped by those in power, shaped by the structure of exchange. And in the end, if performed pain is not felt, the exchange of embodiment fails.

8 (In)Visibility in the Gas Field

Energy from natural gas fuels newer power plants, heats homes, and is a cornerstone of U.S. energy policy. Less polluting than coal, natural gas has been touted as a greener energy source—a "bridge fuel" to wean Americans off more polluting fossil fuels.

There is also an interplay between natural gas and calls for reduced dependence on foreign oil, although at present gasoline and natural gas are not interchangeable. Most vehicles are gasoline powered, so those calls seem misdirected. Nonetheless, the rhetoric in favor of domestic natural gas production makes significant use of this claim.

Any polluting industry is entangled with issues of environmental justice, and natural gas development is no exception. Some people and ecologies will be designated as expendable for whatever outcome is sought. This is particularly the case in political jurisdictions that choose not to employ the precautionary principle and that have limited protective environmental regulations. Residents of natural gas shales in active development have found themselves in this predicament.

This book investigates what happened in one such area, the Barnett Shale in the geographically populated Dallas–Fort Worth metroplex. Industrial activities never meant to coincide have invaded urban and suburban towns and neighborhoods in this region. The impacted population in this case is predominantly white, politically conservative, and middle-class to upper-middle class. Typically speaking, this group has the financial and social capital to avoid harm; however, here they find that their advantages have not been enough. A profitable natural resource lies underneath their homes—a resource that a powerful multi-billion-dollar industry wants to retrieve and control. Although environmental activists fighting against the polluting aspects of the natural gas industry have amassed significant amounts of evidence to support their claims, the practice continues. For an explanation of why that is the case, we can look both to the political history of the region and to the control of knowledge.

Culture and Politics

While I counted out currency in a London pub, a bartender asked me where I was from. "Dallas," I said.

"Who shot JR?" he asked.

Even though ten years had passed since the airing of the final episode of *Dallas* (the remake had yet to happen), the television show, with the mystique and mayhem of Ewing Oil, remained part of the cultural narrative of Texas. I found myself explaining to the bartender that I didn't own a horse, that I didn't own any oil wells, and that I seldom ate beef.

Urban natural gas development is an extension of Texas culture. Independence and self-sufficiency reign, with a legacy of cowboys and oil magnates. The wildcatter was historically a bold, romanticized figure. Fortunes have been made—and continue to be made—from oil and gas. Meanwhile, there has also been a history of resistance to regulation and of clashes between industry and the government. Today, the Texas state government is overwhelmingly Republican, and their policies offer significant support for business and industry.

Springing forth from this history, Texan's are left with an antiquated regulatory system largely based on the needs of rural areas. Legal authority is weak and is fragmented among a multitude of governmental organizations.

Reluctant Activists, Compelled to Act

Most of the activists I spoke with had come to activism reluctantly. They said they felt compelled to act, compelled to try to change the political and cultural environment that supports unfettered urban natural gas development. They often noticed patterns of health problems in their neighborhoods. Through popular epidemiology (Brown 1992, 2007), they linked reports of illness to the industrial activities in their area.

As has already been noted, this group is primarily white, middle-class to upper-middle class, college educated, and politically conservative. They do not view themselves as victims of oppression outside of this issue, and they have little prior experience in social activism. Activism is new to them, and it is not always a comfortable role. They find themselves presented with unexpected barriers. They are learning to navigate the political system— indeed, one participant told me she had to *find* the city hall building first. Participatory democracy is not something they have experience in.

Environmental problems can be a shock to these people, because they are typically sheltered from industrial activities. Used to buying their way to safety (Szasz 2007), they are often not aware of the difficulties of living in proximity to polluting industries.

I was asked why, this being a largely Republican voting base, Republican elected officials weren't doing more to address their concerns. I think this is in part due to that fact that these constituents are new to social activism and participatory democracy. They continue to learn how to be visible, how to navigate the system to get results. And although they have resources, theirs are nothing in comparison with those of the oil and gas industry. Theirs is a difficult battle, and many give up in frustration. Meanwhile the Democratic Party in this region has yet to exploit this to its advantage.

A discussion of how natural gas development affects a populated area raises questions of environmental justice. The people in my research are neither poor nor (for the most part) members of racial or ethnic minority groups. Their communities are nonetheless disproportionally burdened by the negative effects of natural gas development. They are living in a sacrifice zone (Lerner 2012), albeit one that is relatively posh.

A large part of becoming visible in the gas fields involves control over knowledge—the ability to define what is and what isn't a threat to health and the environment. The Barnett Shale discourse is filled with struggles over "facts." The foundations of policy making appear to rest on science; however, as has been shown, the science in question is mutable. Expert knowledge and lay knowledge differ, and even among experts the facts are in dispute. Epistemic privilege therefore is granted to the more powerful groups, and the groups in power try to eliminate all expressions of emotional pain from the discussion.

Toward a Sociology of Community-Level Health Threats

A community-level health threat interrupts day-to-day life and threatens entire communities. Through study of community-level health threats we can examine the meanings and actions of people who have decided that a phenomenon is a threat to their collective health. This is more than an academic exercise. "Local communities in ever-increasing numbers are forced to decide how to act toward and make sense of complicated, value-laden environmental problems," Gunter and Kroll-Smith (2007, 5) write. Real threats—be they polluting industries, infectious disease outbreaks, or natural or human-made disasters—create fear in communities. Through understanding how communities respond to such fear, we can mitigate some of the problems that arise.

The primary trait of a community-level health threat is that anyone in the community could be affected. Perhaps the threat is a polluting industry. Perhaps it is a communicable disease. Perhaps it is radiation exposure. The defining characteristic is that, although some members of the community may be more or less susceptible than others, any of them could experience morbidity or mortality as a result of exposure. Pathology may vary from person to person—where one person may develop a severe lung infection or cancer, another may have mild allergy-like symptoms. Generally speaking, though, anyone in the community is vulnerable. This vulnerability creases a sense of fear, because no one really knows who will be harmed or to what extent, yet they believe a threat is present in their environment. In contrast, an individual health threat affects only one person directly. Perhaps a woman finds a lump in her breast and is frightened about her own health. Perhaps a man goes to his doctor for a cough and an x-ray shows a haze that the physician is concerned about. These are individual diagnoses, health scares that are dealt with individually. Health scares remain individual-level health threats until or unless a cause that threatens others in the community is identified.

Studies have shown that fear over health threats increases as individual control over the hazard decreases. "This may provide a clue for one of the necessary conditions for a putative hazard to become a focus of societal concern," Kabat writes (2008, 13). Hazards that are invisible are frightening, especially when individuals believe something to be a threat while experts tell them they have nothing to fear. When information about a hazard is contested, when facts are in dispute, anxiety rises. "How harmful is this?" people wonder. "Am I at risk? Are my children?"

I have found social representation theory to be an informative framework for understanding response to community-level health threats. Using that framework, we can argue that an object (in this case, a perceived health threat from natural gas drilling) is inserted into the local community, typically without any forewarning. The community then undergoes a process of making sense of that object. This happens through interaction and discourse. Through debate and counter debate. It is dialectical and spiral in nature. Does this object, this perceived threat, fit into the community's knowledge base? How does it fit? If it doesn't, if it is something new, how do people respond? The object in this particular case study is natural gas drilling; however, the object could vary with different scenarios. Perhaps it is a new strain of influenza or an outbreak of some other communicable disease. Maybe it is a polluting chemical or a radiation leak. In any case, the object presents a threat, theoretically to every member of the community.

On the basis of this research, I propose that a community-level health threat can be characterized as follows:

1. There is a flurry of discursive practice after the identification of the object of harm.
2. The response from governmental officials is either minimal or confusing.
3. Perceptions of the event vary, and risk is disputed.
4. Grassroots activity responds to the threat in some manner.
5. Talismans are used to help mitigate the risk.

I have seen these characteristics not only in the case of natural gas drilling but also in my previous epidemiological work on infectious diseases.

Initially, there is a flurry of discursive practice after the identification of the object of harm. At this stage, an object has been identified and has been construed as possibly harmful. What does that mean for the community? What is the proper response? Often this stage is nebulous as community members try to sort through meanings attached to the object.

It is through discursive practice that the social representation of the event is created and managed. Discursive action takes on many forms as people in the community sort through what this event means and what to do about it. Through official and unofficial channels, by formal and informal techniques, the threat is considered. Newspaper articles and editorials are written, online social networking groups emerge and the issues are discussed, friends converse over coffee, pain is performed—all of the various communication channels are utilized, including written, oral, and other performative expressions.

Complicating matters, responses from governmental officials are either scanty or confusing. Communication barriers and differing positions and understandings influence the perceptions of governmental response. Perceptions of events vary and may be contested. One group may argue that the object in question is quite harmful, others that it is safe. There is a break between lived and expert knowledge, and officials are more likely to be on the side of expert knowledge. Their response is interpreted by the community members as disorganized, confused, or uninformed, and their response may result in a legitimation crisis (Habermas 1973) for the officials, as they may be framed as incompetent guardians. They may be seen as doing too little, or occasionally as overstepping their authority and doing too much. Due to the multiplicity of the regulatory system, responses tend to appear haphazard or contradictory, with agencies "tripping over" one another. Fragmentation of authority contributes to a sense that the government has failed and that the residents have been betrayed. All of this sets up the potential for conflict between the public and government agencies.

When members of the community feel that government has not responded, grassroots activity emerges. Grassroots groups seek to find their own answers, typically through a process of public epidemiology (or, at a minimum, a Google search for information). The conclusions drawn by the grassroots groups often differ from those drawn by regulatory officials. Often the perceptions of the risk of the event differ greatly between the two groups, the grassroots groups generally claiming that the risk is greater risk than the regulatory officials claim it is. Members of the grassroots groups gather evidence—proof of the health threat—to spur regulators to fix the problem. They encounter a barrier of epistemic privilege, however, and find response to their concerns lacking.

If members of the public perceive regulators as incompetent, some will decide to do the needed work themselves. Something must be done, and if the government won't do it then some citizens feel that they must do it— for example, they might pay for their own air or water sampling, or bring in their own experts or perhaps lawyers.

Talismans are used to help mitigate the risk. Talismans are physical objects imbued with seemingly magical properties, although their ability to protect the public is usually not nearly as great as their *perceived* ability to protect. In the case of natural gas drilling activism, the most obvious talisman is the oil and gas ordinance, with its setback requirements. Another talisman is the air-monitoring equipment used to identify levels of pollutants. In other cases, such as outbreaks of infectious disease, talismans might include objects such as hand sanitizer, vaccine, or face masks.

Though the details and the specifics may vary, these overarching aspects seem to recur in communities facing health threats.

Industry Perspectives

In writing this story, I do not wish to disrespect the gritty reality of those who work in the gas fields. Theirs is a difficult job, and for every household toxic exposure that may be occurring, the workers are regularly exposed as well—perhaps even more so. One activist told me:

I met with these whistle blowers [gas field workers]. They told me stuff. Oh my gosh! Like they make them go inside those tanker trucks with no protective clothing on and clean those trucks out. After they're hauling flowback. [One worker] said that he has seen these guys who were burned through their leather boots so badly they could hardly walk. Chemical burns the next day. Just really bad. Just from the fumes. Not from actual [contact] with the liquid. Then they got scared and we lost them. They told us they wouldn't go on record.

The natural gas industry extracts, refines, and transports minerals to maximize profits. Members of the public use electricity generated from the burning of those minerals, burn the minerals to heat their homes, and use plastics and other products made from those minerals. Communities are not polluted out of malice, but as a side effect.

I chose not to focus on the industry's side of the experience I describe because my overriding interest, sociologically, is in the social construction of health threats and the community-level response to those threats. Nonetheless, I believe that the industry's perspective is important, and I hope others will take it up in the future as an area of inquiry.

Frack Free Texas

We Americans are addicted to fossil fuels, and we have been unable to wean ourselves off of them. Unfortunately for us, use of fossil fuels pollutes the environment, and we have been unable to find a way around that problem.

Despite the benefits of the natural gas industry (such as job creation and moving away from coal as a fuel source), communities in which extraction activities are under way also cope with associated pollution and other negative consequences.

As I was writing this book, activists in the city of Denton won a significant victory in their fight against urban natural gas activities, and Denton become the first city in Texas to ban hydraulic fracturing.

A grassroots organization called the Denton Drilling Awareness Group amassed thousands of signatures on a petition calling for a ballot measure to ban fracking within the city limits. In November of 2014 the ban was put to a vote, in which it prevailed overwhelmingly despite an intensive pro-industry campaign. One pro-drilling organization, Denton Taxpayers, purportedly spent about $700,000 fighting the measure, using funds largely donated by natural gas companies (Heinkel-Wolfe 2014).

In response to the outcome of the vote, the Texas Railroad Commissioner said that "he was disappointed that voters 'fell prey to scare tactics and mischaracterizations of the truth in passing the hydraulic fracturing ban'" (Baker 2014). Denton's mayor, on the other hand, defended the voters' choice and proclaimed that the city would "exercise the legal remedies that are available to us should the ordinance be challenged" (Baker 2014).

While passing the ban, the voters of Denton also elected a slate of Republican candidates into office.

A lawsuit challenging the ban was filed by noon the day after the vote.

References

Absher, Brandon. 2012. Toward a Concept of Ecological Violence: Martin Heidegger and Mountain Justice. *Radical Philosophy Review* 15 (1): 89–101.

Aldrich, Tim, and Thomas Sinks. 2002. Things to Know and Do about Cancer Clusters. *Cancer Investigation* 20 (5, 6): 810–816.

American Lung Association (ALA). 2011. State of the Air. http://www.stateoftheair.org/.

Andrews, Anthony, Peter Folger, and Marc Humphries. 2009. *Unconventional Gas Shales: Development, Technology, and Policy Issues.* Washington: Congressional Research Service.

American Lung Association (ALA). 2011. "State of the Air." http://www.stateoftheair.org/.

Armendariz, Al. 2009. Emissions from Natural Gas Productions in the Barnett Shale Area and Opportunities for Cost-Effective Improvements. http://www.edf.org/sites/default/files/9235_Barnett_Shale_Report.pdf.

Baker, Max B. 2014. Denton Votes Approve State's First Ban on Hydraulic Fracturing. *Fort Worth Star Telegram*, November 4, 2014 (http://www.star-telegram.com/2014/11/04/6260352/denton-voters-approving-fracking.html).

Baker, Rick, and Mike Pring. 2009. Drilling Rig Emission Inventory for the State of Texas, Final Report. http://www.tceq.state.tx.us/assets/public/implementation/air/am/contracts/reports/ei/5820783985FY0901-20090715-ergi-Drilling_Rig_EI.pdf.

Bellec, Stéphanie, Dénis Hemon, and Jacqueline Clavel. 2005. Answering Cluster Investigation Requests: The Value of Simple Simulations and Statistical Tools. *European Journal of Epidemiology* 20: 663–671.

Boxall, Peter C., Wing H. Chan, and Melville L. McMillan. 2005. The Impact of Oil and Natural Gas Facilities on Rural Residential Property Values: A Spatial Hedonic Analysis. *Resource and Energy Economics* 27: 248–269.

Bradford, Carrie, Tina Walker, Natalie Archer, Susan Prosperie, Ben Blount, and John F. Villanaccie. 2010. *Final Report, DISH, Texas Exposure Investigation, DISH, Denton County, Texas*. Austin: Texas Department of State Health Services.

Brody, Samuel D., B. Mitchell Peck, and Wesley E. Highfield. 2004. Examining Localized Patterns of Air Quality Perception in Texas: A Spatial and Statistical Analysis. *Risk Analysis* 24 (6): 1561–1574.

Brosh, Allie. 2013. Boyfriend Doesn't Have Ebola. Probably. http://hyperboleandahalf .blogspot.com/2010/02/boyfriend-doesnt-have-ebola-probably.html.

Brown, Phil. 1992. Popular Epidemiology and Toxic Waste Contamination: Lay and Professional Ways of Knowing. *Journal of Health and Social Behavior* 33 (3): 267–281.

Brown, Phil. 2007. *Toxic Exposures: Contested Illnesses and the Environmental Health Movement*. New York: Columbia University Press.

Butler-Kisber, Lynn. 2010. *Qualitative Inquiry: Thematic, Narrative and Arts-Informed Perspectives*. London: SAGE.

Charman, Karen. 2010. Trashing the Planet for Natural Gas: Shale Gas Development Threatens Freshwater Sources, Likely Escalates Climate Destabilization. *Capitalism Nature Socialism* 21 (4): 72–82.

Charmaz, Kathy. 2011. Grounded Theory Methods in Social Justice Research. In *The SAGE Handbook of Qualitative Research*, fourth edition, ed. N. K. Denzin and Y. S. Lincoln. Los Angeles: SAGE.

Charmaz, Kathy. 2006. *Constructing Grounded Theory: A Practical Guide to Qualitative Analysis*. New York: SAGE.

Childs, William R. 2005. *The Texas Railroad Commission*. College Station: Texas A&M University Press.

Clark, James Anthony. 1955. *East Texas Oil Fields . . . the first 25 years*. Dallas: Texas Mid-Continent Oil and Gas Association.

Colborn, Theo, Carol Kwistkowski, Kim Schultz, and Mary Bachran. 2011. Natural Gas Operations from a Public Health Perspective. *Human and Ecological Risk Assessment* 17 (5): 1039–1056.

Cole, Luke, and Shiela R. Foster. 2001. *From the Ground Up: Environmental Racism and the Rise of the Environmental Justice Movement*. New York University Press.

Cook Children's Community-Wide Children's Health Assessment and Planning Survey. 2009. Distribution of Childhood Asthma by County. http://www .cookchildrens.org/SiteCollectionDocuments/Pulmonology/asthma/KID_BITS _9_Distribution_of_Childhood_Asthma_by_County_10.1.pdf.

Cox, Mike. 2012. *Historical Photos of Texas Oil*. Nashville: Turner.

Davis, Devra. 2002. *When Smoke Ran Like Water: Tales of Environmental Deception and the Battle Against Pollution*. New York: Basic Books.

Davison, C., G. D. Smith, and S. Frankel. 1991. Lay Epidemiology and the Prevention Paradox: The Implications of Coronary Candidacy for Health Education. *Sociology of Health & Illness* 13 (1): 1–19.

Deffeyes, Kenneth S. 2005. *Beyond Oil: The View From Hubbert's Peak*. New York: Hill and Wang.

Denton County Oil and Gas Task Force Summary Report. 2005. http://www.lyco.org/LinkClick.aspx?fileticket=TSsZQfVbHbs%3D&tabid=516&mid=980.

Denzin, Norman K. 2003. *Performance Ethnography: Critical Pedagogy and the Politics of Culture*. Thousand Oaks: SAGE.

Denzin, Norman K. 2011. *The Qualitative Manifesto: A Call to Arms*. Walnut Creek: Left Coast.

Department of State Health Services (DSHS). 2010. Dish, Tx Exposure Investigation May 2010 Community Meeting. http://www.dshs.state.tx.us/workArea/DownloadAsset.aspx?id=8589956899.

DiGiulio, Dominic C., Richard T. Wilkin, Carlyle Miller, and Gregory Oberley. 2011, *Investigation of Ground Water Contamination Near Pavillion, Wyoming*. Ada: Office of Research and Development National Risk Management Research Laboratory; http://www2.epa.gov/sites/production/files/documents/EPA_ReportOnPavillion_Dec-8-2011.pdf.

Duneier, Mitchell. 1999. *Sidewalk*. New York: Farrar, Straus and Giroux.

Duneier, Mitchell. 2012. How Not to Lie with Ethnography. *Sociological Methodology* 41 (1): 1–11.

Dunlap, Riley E. 2002. Environmental Sociology: A Personal Perspective on Its First Quarter Century. *Organization & Environment* 15: 10–29.

Durkheim, Emile. 1912 [1995]. *The Elementary Forms of Religious Life*, tr. K. E. Fields. New York: Free Press.

Edelstein, Michael R. 2003. Contamination: The Invisible Built Environment. In *Handbook of Environmental Psychology*, ed. Robert B. Bechtel and Arza Churchman. New York: Wiley.

Edelstein, Michael R. 2004. *Contaminated Communities: Coping with Residential Toxic Exposure*, second edition. Boulder: Westview.

EnergyFromShale. 2013. http://www.energyfromshale.org/hydraulic-fracturing/texas-natural-gas.

Figueroa, Robert Melchoir. 2006. Evaluating Environmental Justice Claims. In *Forging Environmentalism: Justice, Livelihood, and Contested Environments*, ed. Joanne Bauer. Armonk: Sharpe.

Finkle, Madelon L., and Adam Law. 2011. The Rush to Drill for Natural Gas: A Public Health Cautionary Tale. *American Journal of Public Health* 101 (5): 784–785.

Flyvbjerg, Bent. 2001. *Making Social Science Matter: Why Social Inquiry Fails and How It Can Succeed Again*, tr. S. Sampson. Cambridge University Press.

Foucault, Michel. [1961] 1965. *Madness and Civilization*, tr. R. H. Tavistock. New York: Pantheon Books.

Foucault, Michel. [1971] 1972. *The Archaeology of Knowledge and the Discourse on Language*, tr. A. M. Sheridan Smith. New York: Pantheon Books.

Gibbs, Lois. 2007. Foreword. In *Toxic Exposures: Contested Illnesses and the Environmental Health Movement*, ed. Phil Brown. New York: Columbia University Press.

Goffman, Erving. 1959. *The Presentation of Self in Everyday Life*. Garden City: Doubleday Anchor.

Goodell, Jeff. 2007. *Big Coal: The Dirty Secret Behind America's Energy Future*. Boston: Houghton Mifflin.

Goodell, Jeff. 2012. The Big Fracking Bubble: The Scam Behind the Gas Boom. *Rolling Stone*, March 15 (http://www.rollingstong.com/politics/news/the-big-fracking-bubble-the-scam-behind-the-gas-boom).

Goodwyn, Lawrence. 1996. *Texas Oil, American Dreams*. Austin: Texas State Historical Association.

Grebowicz, Margret, and Helen Merrick. 2013. *Beyond the Cyborg: Adventures with Donna Haraway*. New York: Columbia University Press.

Gullion, Jessica Smartt. 2002. Complexity and Public Policy Analysis: Texas Welfare Reform and Trends in Teen Births. PhD dissertation, Texas Woman's University.

Gullion, Jessica Smartt. 2013. Toxic Neighborhood. *Qualitative Inquiry* 19 (7): 491–492.

Gullion, Jessica Smartt. 2014. *October Birds: A Novel about Pandemic Influenza, Infection Control, and First Responders*. Rotterdam: Sense.

Gullion, Jessica Smartt, Lisa Henry, and Greg Gullion. 2008. Deciding to Opt Out of Childhood Vaccination Mandates. *Public Health Nursing* 25 (5): 401–408.

Gullion, Jessica, Naomi Meiers, and Rhonda Love. 2011. A Perspective on Health and Natural Gas Operations: A Report for the Denton City Council. White paper presented to City of Denton Natural Gas Taskforce and the Denton City Council, December 21.

Gunter, Valeria, and Steve Kroll-Smith. 2007. *Volatile Places: A Sociology of Communities and Environmental Controversies*. Thousand Oaks: SAGE.

Habermas, Jürgen. 1973. *Legitimation Crisis*, tr. T. McCarthy. Boston: Beacon.

Heinkel-Wolfe, Peggy. 2011. Breast Cancer Rate Climbs Up. *Denton Record Chronicle*, August 31, 2011(http://www.dentonrc.com/local-news/special-projects/gas-well -drilling-headlines/20110831-breast-cancer-rate-climbs-up.ece).

Heinkel-Wolfe, Peggy. 2014. Denton Voters Pass Proposition with 59 Percent. *Denton Record Chronicle*, November 5, 2014 (http://www.dentonrc.com/local-news/local -news-headlines/20141105-fracking-banned.ece).

Horlacher, James Levi. 1929. *A Year in the Oil Fields*. Lexington: Press of the Kentucky Kernel.

Howarth, Robert W., Renee Santoro, and Anthony Ingraffea. 2011. Methane and the Greenhouse-Gas Footprint of Natural Gas from Shale Formation. *Climatic Change* 106: 679–690.

Huffington Post. 2009. Gov. Rick Perry: Texas Could Secede, Leave Union. Editorial, *Huffington Post* (http://www.huffingtonpost.com/2009/04/15/gov-rick-perry-texas -coul_n_187490.html).

Jackson, Robert B., Brooks Rainey Pearson, Stephen G. Osborn, Nathaniel R. Warner, and Avner Vengosh. 2012. Research and Policy Recommendations for Hydraulic Fracturing and Shale-Gas Extraction. https://nicholas.duke.edu/cgc/Hydraulic FracturingWhitepaper2011.pdf.

Javers, Eamon. 2011. Oil Executive: Military-Style "Psyops" Experience Applied. http://www.cnbc.com/id/45208498.

Johnson, Renee J., and Michael J. Scicchitano. 2012. Don't Call Me NIMBY: Public Attitudes Toward Solid Waste Facilities. *Environment and Behavior* 22: 410–426.

Kabat, Geoffrey C. 2008. *Hyping Health Risks: Environmental Hazards in Daily Life and the Science of Epidemiology*. New York: Columbia University Press.

Keeling, Arn, and John Sandlos. 2009. Environmental Justice Goes Underground? Historical Notes from Canada's Northern Mining Frontier. *Environmental Justice* 2 (3): 117–125.

Klare, Michael T. 2012. The New Fossil Fuel Fever. *Nation* 294 (12): 15–22.

Koffler, Shelley. 2012. Texas' Legal Battles Likely to Continue with Obama's Reelection. http://keranews.org/post/texas-legal-battles-likely-continue-obamas-reelection.

Lal, Jayati. 1999. Situating Locations and the Politics of Self, Identity, and "Other" in Living and Writing the Text. In *Feminist Approaches to Theory and Methodology:*

An Interdisciplinary Reader, ed. S. Hesse-Biber, C. Gilmartin, and R. Lyndenberg. Oxford University Press.

Langston, Nancy. 2010. *Toxic Bodies: Hormone Disruptors and the Legacy of DES*. New Haven: Yale University Press.

Lather, Patti. 2010. *Engaging Science Policy from the Side of the Messy*. New York: Lang.

Latour, Bruno. 2010. *On the Modern Cult of the Factish Gods*. Durham: Duke University Press.

Leavy, Patricia. 2009. *Method Meets Art: Arts-Based Research Practice*. New York: Guilford.

Lerner, Steve. 2012. *Sacrifice Zones: The Front Lines of Toxic Chemical Exposures in the United States*. Cambridge: MIT Press.

Littig, Beate. 2001. *Feminist Perspectives on Environment and Society*. Harlow: Pearson Education.

Madden, Raymond. 2010. *Being Ethnographic: A Guide to the Theory and Practice of Ethnography*. Los Angeles: SAGE.

Madison, D. Soyini. 2012. *Critical Ethnography: Method, Ethics, and Performance*, second edition. Los Angeles: SAGE.

Malinowski, Bronislaw. 1922. *Argonauts of the Western Pacific: An Account of Native Enterprise and Adventure in the Archipelagos of Melanesian New Guinea*. London: Routledge.

Mangan, Frank J. 1977. *The Pipeliners*. El Paso: Guynes.

Margonelli, Lisa. 2007. *Oil on the Brain: Petroleum's Long, Strange Trip to Your Tank*. New York: Broadway Books.

McGraw, Seamus. 2011. *The End of Country*. New York: Random House.

McKenzie, Lisa M., Roxana Z. Witter, Lee S. Newman, and John L. Adgate. 2012. Human Health Risk Assessment of Air Emissions from Development of Unconventional Natural Gas Resources. *Science of the Total Environment* 424: 79–87.

Mills, C. Wright. 1959. *The Sociological Imagination*. Oxford University Press.

Mortimer-Sandilands, Catriona, and Bruce Erickson. 2010. *Queer Ecologies: Sex, Nature, Politics, Desire*. Bloomington: Indiana University Press.

Moscovici, Serge. 1963. Attitudes and Opinions. *Annual Review of Psychology* 14: 231–260.

Murray, Michael. 2002. Connecting Narrative and Social Representation Theory in Health Research. *Social Sciences Information. Information Sur les Sciences Sociales* 41 (4): 653–673.

Nancarrow, Heather, Stewart Lockie, and Sanjay Sharma. 2009. Intimate Partner Abuse of Women in a Central Queensland Mining Region. http://www.aic.gov.au/publications/current%20series/tandi/361-380/tandi378.html.

Nichols, Nancy A. 2008. *Lake Effect: Two Sisters and a Town's Toxic Legacy*. Washington: Island.

Orta-Martinez, Marti, and Matt Finer. 2010. Oil Frontiers and Indigenous Resistance in the Peruvian Amazon. *Ecological Economics* 70: 207–218.

Osborn, Stephen G., Avner Vengosh, Nathaniel R. Warner, and Robert B. Jackson. 2011. Methane Contamination of Drinking Water Accompanying Gas-Well and Hydraulic Fracturing. *Proceedings of the National Academy of Sciences* 108 (20): 8172–8176 (http://www.pnas.org/content/early/2011/05/02/1100682108.full.pdf+html).

Pascale, Celine-Marie. 2011. *Cartographies of Knowledge: Exploring Qualitative Epistemologies*. London: SAGE.

Pezzullo, Phaedra C. 2007. *Toxic Tourism: Rhetorics of Pollution, Travel, and Environmental Justice*. Tuscaloosa: University of Alabama Press.

Potter, J., and D. Edwards. 1999. Social Representations and Discursive Psychology: From Cognition to Action. *Culture and Psychology* 5: 447–458.

Rahm, Dianne. 2011. Regulating Hydraulic Fracturing in Shale Gas Plays: The Case of Texas. *Energy Policy* 39: 2974–2981.

Revkin, Andrew C. 2012. When Publicity Precedes Peer Review in the Fight Over Gas Impacts. http://dotearth.blogs.nytimes.com/2012/07/25.

Richards, Sam. 2010. A Radical Experience in Empathy. http://www.youtube.com/watch?v=kUEGHdQO7WA.

Riley, G. A., and D. Baah-Odoom. 2010. Do stigma, blame and stereotyping contribute to unsafe sexual behaviour? A test of claims about the spread of HIV/AIDS arising from social representation theory and the AIDS risk reduction model. *Social Science & Medicine* 71: 600–607.

Savin-Baden, Maggi, and Claire Howell Major. 2013. *Qualitative Research: The Essential Guide to Theory and Practice*. London: Routledge.

Schmidt, Charles W. 2011. Blind Rush? Shale Gas Boom Proceeds Amid Human Health Questions. *Environmental Health Perspectives* 119 (8): A348–A353.

Schwandt, Thomas. 2008. Toward a Practical Theory of Evidence for Evaluation. In *Credible Evidence in Evaluation and Applied Research*, ed. S. Donaldson, C. Christie, and M. Mark. Thousand Oaks: SAGE.

Sharma, Sanjay. 2009. An Exploration into the Wellbeing of the Families Living in the "Suburbs in the Bush." *Australian and New Zealand Journal of Public Health* 33 (3): 262–269.

Shiva, Vandana. 2002. *Water Wars: Privatization, Pollution, and Profit*. Cambridge: South End Press.

Shiva, Vandana. 2009. Soil Not Oil: Environmental Justice in an Age of Climate Crisis. *Alternatives Journal* 35 (3): 19–23.

Spiegel, Samuel. 2009. Occupational Health, Mercury Exposure, and Environmental Justice: Learning from Experiences in Tanzania. *American Journal of Public Health* 99 (S3): S550–S558.

State Impact. 2013. A Look at Natural Gas Production in Texas. http://stateimpact .npr.org/texas/tag/natural-gas-production-in-texas/.

Steingraber, Sandra. 2011. *Raising Elijah: Protecting Our Children in an Age of Environmental Crisis*. Philadelphia: Da Capo.

St. Pierre, Elizabeth Adams. 2011. Post Qualitative Research: The Critique and the Coming After. In *The SAGE Handbook of Qualitative Research*. fourth edition, ed. N. K. Denzin and Y. S. Lincoln. Thousand Oaks: SAGE.

Stretesky, Paul B., and Michael J. Lynch. 2011. Coal Strip Mining, Mountaintop Removal, and the Distribution of Environmental Violations across the United States, 2002–2008. *Landscape Research* 36 (2): 209–230.

Szasz, Andrew. 2007. *Shopping Our Way to Safety: How We Changed from Protecting the Environment to Protecting Ourselves*. Minneapolis: University of Minnesota Press.

Texas Commission on Environmental Quality (TCEQ). 2013a. About Effects Screening Levels (ESLs). http://www.tceq.texas.gov/toxicology/esl.

Texas Commission on Environmental Quality. 2013b. TCEQ Strategic Plan, Fiscal Years 2013–2017. http://www.tceq.texas.gov/publications/sfr/035-13.html.

Texas Railroad Commission. 2013. Newark, East (Barnett Shale) Field. http:// www.rrc.state.tx.us/data/fielddata/barnettshale.pdf.

Town of Dish v. Atmos Energy et al. 2011. http://www.shaledigest.com/documents/ legal/Dish%20v%20Atmos%20et%20al.pdf.

Tuhus, Melinda. 2011. Fracked to Pieces. *E-The Environmental Magazine*, November 1: 20–30.

United Nations Environment Programme (UNEP). 1992. Rio Declaration on Environmental Development. http://www.unep.org/Documents.Multilingual/Default .asp?documentid=78&articleid=1163.

Urkidi, Leire, and Mariana Walter. 2011. Dimensions of Environmental Justice in Anti-Gold Mining Movements in Latin America. *Geoforum* 42: 683–695.

van der Horst, Dan. 2007. NIMBY or not? Exploring the Relevance of Location and the Politics of Voiced Opinions in Renewable Energy Siting Controversies. *Energy Policy* 35: 2705–2714.

Walraven, Bill, and Marjorie K. Walraven. 2005. *Wooden Rigs—Iron Men: The Story of Oil and Gas in South Texas*. Corpus Christi Geological Society.

We Are Power Shift. 2012. Death Thanks the Denton, TX Gas Well Task Force. http://www.wearepowershift.org/blogs/death-thanks-denton-tx-gas-well-task-force.

Weber, Max. 1930 [1958]. *The Protestant Ethic and the Spirit of Capitalism*, tr. T. Parsons. New York: Scribner

Westbrook, David A. 2008. *Navigators of the Contemporary: Why Ethnography Matters*. University of Chicago Press.

Whiteside, Kerry H. 2006. *Precautionary Politics: Principle and Practice in Confronting Environmental Risk*. Cambridge: MIT Press.

Wilber, Tom. 2012. *Under the Surface: Fracking, Fortunes, and the Fate of the Marcellus Shale*. Ithaca: Cornell University Press.

Williams, Laura, Margaret A. Honein, and Sonja A. Rasmussen. 2002. Methods for a Public Health Response to Birth Defects Clusters. *Teratology* 66: 330–350.

Wilson, Sharon. 2014. Psyops. *Bluedaze Drilling Reform*. http://www.texassharon.com/category/psyops.

Wilson, Sharon, Lisa Sumi, Bill Walker, and Jennifer Goldman. 2011. *Natural Gas Flowback: How the Texas Natural Gas Book Affects Health and Safety*. http://www.earthworksaction.org/files/publications/FLOWBACK-TXOGAP-HealthReport-lowres.pdf.

Witter, Roxanna, Kaylan Stinson, Holly Sackett, Stefanie Putter, Gregory Kinney, Daniel Teitelbaum, and Lee Newman. 2008. Potential Exposure-Related Human Health Effects of Oil and Gas Developmen. White paper, Colorado School of Public Health. http://docs.nrdc.org/health/files/hea_08091702A.pdf.

Wundt, Wilhelm. 1916. *Elements of Folk Psychology*. London: Allen & Unwin. Available at http://psychclassics.asu.edu/Wundt/Folk/intro.htm.

Yardley, Jim. 2001. For Texas Now, Water and Not Oil Is Gold. *New York Times*, April 16 (http://www.nytimes.com/2001/04/16/us/for-texas-now-water-and-not-oil-is-liquid-gold.htm).

Index

Urban and Industrial Environments

series editor: Robert Gottlieb, Henry R. Luce Professor of Urban and Environmental Policy, Occidental College

Maureen Smith, *The U.S. Paper Industry and Sustainable Production: An Argument for Restructuring*

Keith Pezzoli, *Human Settlements and Planning for Ecological Sustainability: The Case of Mexico City*

Sarah Hammond Creighton, *Greening the Ivory Tower: Improving the Environmental Track Record of Universities, Colleges, and Other Institutions*

Jan Mazurek, *Making Microchips: Policy, Globalization, and Economic Restructuring in the Semiconductor Industry*

William A. Shutkin, *The Land That Could Be: Environmentalism and Democracy in the Twenty-First Century*

Richard Hofrichter, ed., *Reclaiming the Environmental Debate: The Politics of Health in a Toxic Culture*

Robert Gottlieb, *Environmentalism Unbound: Exploring New Pathways for Change*

Kenneth Geiser, *Materials Matter: Toward a Sustainable Materials Policy*

Thomas D. Beamish, *Silent Spill: The Organization of an Industrial Crisis*

Matthew Gandy, *Concrete and Clay: Reworking Nature in New York City*

David Naguib Pellow, *Garbage Wars: The Struggle for Environmental Justice in Chicago*

Julian Agyeman, Robert D. Bullard, and Bob Evans, eds., *Just Sustainabilities: Development in an Unequal World*

Barbara L. Allen, *Uneasy Alchemy: Citizens and Experts in Louisiana's Chemical Corridor Disputes*

Dara O'Rourke, *Community-Driven Regulation: Balancing Development and the Environment in Vietnam*

Brian K. Obach, *Labor and the Environmental Movement: The Quest for Common Ground*

Peggy F. Barlett and Geoffrey W. Chase, eds., *Sustainability on Campus: Stories and Strategies for Change*

Steve Lerner, *Diamond: A Struggle for Environmental Justice in Louisiana's Chemical Corridor*

Jason Corburn, *Street Science: Community Knowledge and Environmental Health Justice*

Peggy F. Barlett, ed., *Urban Place: Reconnecting with the Natural World*

David Naguib Pellow and Robert J. Brulle, eds., *Power, Justice, and the Environment: A Critical Appraisal of the Environmental Justice Movement*

Eran Ben-Joseph, *The Code of the City: Standards and the Hidden Language of Place Making*

Nancy J. Myers and Carolyn Raffensperger, eds., *Precautionary Tools for Reshaping Environmental Policy*

Kelly Sims Gallagher, *China Shifts Gears: Automakers, Oil, Pollution, and Development*

Kerry H. Whiteside, *Precautionary Politics: Principle and Practice in Confronting Environmental Risk*

Ronald Sandler and Phaedra C. Pezzullo, eds., *Environmental Justice and Environmentalism: The Social Justice Challenge to the Environmental Movement*

Julie Sze, *Noxious New York: The Racial Politics of Urban Health and EnvironmentalJustice*

Robert D. Bullard, ed., *Growing Smarter: Achieving Livable Communities, Environmental Justice, and Regional Equity*

Ann Rappaport and Sarah Hammond Creighton, *Degrees That Matter: Climate Change and the University*

Michael Egan, *Barry Commoner and the Science of Survival: The Remaking of American Environmentalism*

David J. Hess, *Alternative Pathways in Science and Industry: Activism, Innovation, and the Environment in an Era of Globalization*

Peter F. Cannavò, *The Working Landscape: Founding, Preservation, and the Politics of Place*

Paul Stanton Kibel, ed., *Rivertown: Rethinking Urban Rivers*

Kevin P. Gallagher and Lyuba Zarsky, *The Enclave Economy: Foreign Investment and Sustainable Development in Mexico's Silicon Valley*

David N. Pellow, *Resisting Global Toxics: Transnational Movements for Environmental Justice*

Robert Gottlieb, *Reinventing Los Angeles: Nature and Community in the Global City*

David V. Carruthers, ed., *Environmental Justice in Latin America: Problems, Promise, and Practice*

Tom Angotti, *New York for Sale: Community Planning Confronts Global Real Estate*

Paloma Pavel, ed., *Breakthrough Communities: Sustainability and Justice in the Next American Metropolis*

Anastasia Loukaitou-Sideris and Renia Ehrenfeucht, *Sidewalks: Conflict and Negotiation over Public Space*

David J. Hess, *Localist Movements in a Global Economy: Sustainability, Justice, and Urban Development in the United States*

Julian Agyeman and Yelena Ogneva-Himmelberger, eds., *Environmental Justice and Sustainability in the Former Soviet Union*

Jason Corburn, *Toward the Healthy City: People, Places, and the Politics of Urban Planning*

JoAnn Carmin and Julian Agyeman, eds.,*Environmental Inequalities Beyond Borders: Local Perspectives on Global Injustices*

Louise Mozingo, *Pastoral Capitalism: A History of Suburban Corporate Landscapes*

Gwen Ottinger and Benjamin Cohen, eds., *Technoscience and Environmental Justice: Expert Cultures in a Grassroots Movement*

Samantha MacBride, *Recycling Reconsidered: The Present Failure and Future Promise of Environmental Action in the United States*

Andrew Karvonen, *Politics of Urban Runoff: Nature, Technology, and the Sustainable City*

Daniel Schneider, *Hybrid Nature: Sewage Treatment and the Contradictions of the Industrial Ecosystem*

Catherine Tumber, *Small, Gritty, and Green: The Promise of America's Smaller Industrial Cities in a Low-Carbon World*

Sam Bass Warner and Andrew H. Whittemore, *American Urban Form: A Representative History*

John Pucher and Ralph Buehler, eds., *City Cycling*

Stephanie Foote and Elizabeth Mazzolini, eds., *Histories of the Dustheap: Waste, Material Cultures, Social Justice*

David J. Hess, *Good Green Jobs in a Global Economy: Making and Keeping New Industries in the United States*

Joseph F. C. DiMento and Clifford Ellis, *Changing Lanes: Visions and Histories of Urban Freeways*

Joanna Robinson, *Contested Water: The Struggle Against Water Privatization in the United States and Canada*

William B. Meyer, *The Environmental Advantages of Cities: Countering Commonsense Antiurbanism*

Rebecca L. Henn and Andrew J. Hoffman, eds., *Constructing Green: The Social Structures of Sustainability*

Peggy F. Barlett and Geoffrey W. Chase, eds., *Sustainability in Higher Education: Stories and Strategies for Transformation*

Isabelle Anguelovski, *Neighborhood as Refuge: Community Reconstruction, Place-Remaking, and Environmental Justice in the City*

Kelly Sims Gallagher, *The Global Diffusion of Clean Energy Technology: Lessons from China*

Vinit Mukhija and Anastasia Loukaitou-Sideris, eds., *The Informal City: Settings, Strategies, Responses*

Roxanne Warren, *Rail and the City: Shrinking Our Carbon Footprint and Reimagining Urban Space*

Marianne Krasny and Keith Tidball, *Civic Ecology: Adaptation and Transformation from the Ground Up*

Julian Agyeman and Duncan McLaren, *Sharing Cities: Enhancing Equity, Rebuilding Community, and Cutting Resource Use*

Jessica Smartt Gullion, *Fracking the Neighborhood: Reluctant Activists and Natural Gas Drilling*